When a man or a wom........,
the soul rises to the upper reaches
and settles at the root of their Own Tree.
In time, the soul descends into the valley
and enters the breast of a baby about to be born.

'Memento Poem', Kenzaburō Ōe

mpT
MODERN POETRY IN TRANSLATION
The best of world poetry

No. 2 2025
© Modern Poetry in Translation 2025 and contributors

ISSN (print) 0969-3572
ISSN (online) 2052-3017
ISBN (print) 978-1-910485-42-2

Printed and bound in Great Britain by Typecast Colour, Kent
For submissions and subscriptions please visit
www.modernpoetryintranslation.com

Modern Poetry in Translation Limited. A Company Limited by Guarantee
Registered in England and Wales, Number 5881603 UK
Registered Charity Number 1118223

Supported using public funding by
ARTS COUNCIL
ENGLAND
LOTTERY FUNDED

The Fenton
Arts Trust

Cover description: The cover has a dark blue background with a paler blue image of low hills with flat grassland on the lower third of the page. On the right is a large white and pale-blue image of a long thin plant with five leaves and some small flowers at the top. It reaches about three-quarters of the way up the page, framing the cover. On the left is a similar sized pale blue-and-white image of bent grass, with some leaning towards the centre of the page as if blown by the wind. This image spreads onto the back page where there are also two smaller pale blue images of leaves.

Above: On the left, the Arts Council England logo curves around in a circle, next to a black outline of a hand crossing fingers. Underneath both images, 'LOTTERY FUNDED' is written. In a line on the right, the text reads, 'Supported using public funding by ARTS COUNCIL ENGLAND'.

On the right, the Fenton Arts Trust logo contains the words 'The Fenton Arts Trust' in black on a white background. Above the word 'The' there is a black heraldic fleur-de-lis image, which represents a three-petalled lily flower bound with a horizontal band.

MODERN POETRY IN TRANSLATION

Rhythms of the Land
Focus on the Poetry of Nature

CONTENTS

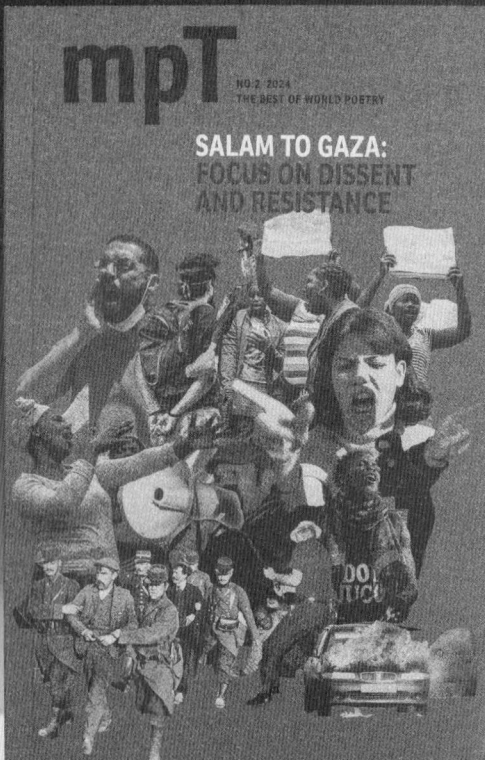

EDITORIAL

By Jessica Sequeira, Guest Editor

What is the music of the earth? How can poetry listen to the cycles and
seasons of nature, the sounds of water and wind? What stories might
the rivers and forests tell, what are their histories and memories?
In the current issue of *Modern Poetry in Translation*, we looked for
translated work that explores the theme of 'rhythms of the land'. We
welcomed poems related to ecology, climate change, mythologies that
respect the earth, correspondences between outer territory and inner
self, and the cultivation of a slow, nurturing relation with commu-
nities and other beings, in contrast to the acceleration and violence of
the news cycle. The poems we chose take diverse perspectives in their
focus on the poetry of nature, incorporating plant, animal and human
elements to praise or criticise modern life. Birth and death appear
often, with the significance of the human entrance into the world and
the passage away from it forming part of the dynamics of natural
processes. An idea of the continued existence of the sentient also
underpins many of the poems, a reincarnation of the material into
new forms that one hopes can occur with gentleness rather than
distress. Violence occurs as an abrupt assault on the dignity of the
material, a failure to respect history and create with tenderness.

For Cindy A. Velasquez (trans. Alton Melvar M. Dapanas), the
deaths of chickens mark the rhythms of the seasons, and in the
aftermath of the pain of a betrayal, a woman's tears flow into the ocean
and through the womb, in a continuity of the human with the natural.
In the work of Claudia Magliano (trans. Jesse Lee Kercheval and
Jeannine Marie Pitas), the violence of meat production is made
explicit through a cycle focused on the cow. Dalia Taha (trans. Sara
Elkamel) writes poems centred on small, affectionate moments within
nature that contrast with this devastating moment of violence in
Palestine, in which military force is obliterating the lives of so many

innocent civilians. A poem by Kenzaburō Ōe (trans. Akagi Kobayashi) reveals another facet of the work of the Nobel prize winner, known for his novels, through the profound connection to his ancestral village with its ancient forests, which illuminates not only his writing but also his political work campaigning against nuclear power. The poems of Maarja Pärtna (trans. Hilary Bird) are intimate portraits of domestic life that maintain an awareness of historical change. Elena Salamanca (trans. Ryan Greene) roots her work in family history and the experiences of women's bodies that cross generations, from caring for a child with neonatal tetanus to undergoing a hysterectomy, which interweave with the natural histories of volcanoes and other forces of nature, as an alternative to predominating, top-down histories of the nation-state. Håkan Sandell (trans. Bill Coyle) composes hymns to the earth that bring the 'I' into the song of creation. Marina Tsvetaeva (trans. Stephen Capus), another familiar figure of literary history, also appears here from a different angle, in her lonely communion with nature, as in exile she leans over the wood of her writing desk—the next life of a tree. Piedad Bonnett (trans. Richard Gwyn) channels anxiety and post-modern isolation in her poems, in which the individual body is often disconnected from those of others, but also the deep sensuality of the universe, with its geometries of stars and secret meanings, in which a person can become a flower blossoming into words. The poems of Yan Li (trans. Anna Yin) suggest gaps beyond language that might hold the remnants of old cosmos, the enigmatic seeds of what is to come. Emi Miyaoka (self-translated) presents a vision that is musical, fantastical and playfully curious, featuring flying cats, a promise of what the future might bring. Begoña Ugalde (trans. Drago Yurac) confesses her heart to be an active volcano, and conceives of writing as an intuitive archaeology, in which verses change state just as matter does. The poems of Gabriela Ruivo (trans. Gilles Madan) have to do with the blurring of the edges of experience, people who are birds or dream of being birds, trees that experience the expansion of their boundaries and the possibilities of infinity. Rifat Abbas, Ashu Lal, Sanwal Gurmani and Tauqir Reza (trans. Mediah Ahmed) form part of the wondrous selection 'Nature's rhythmical rebellions, the musical resistances of the fields, rivers and skies', poems that insist on slower rhythms and meaningful relationships amidst bomb blasts, the smoke of motorcars, the so-called miracles of technology, systemic violence and absence of any perceptible deity; they continue to marvel at the ecological and ethereal, the green thread of life. Ali Asadollahi (self-translated) dedicates her poem to a lake, which is full of love, but also expresses anguish at environmental destruction and frustration at the silence that prevails. The poem by N.S. Sigogo (trans. Stephen Walsh) is a breath of fresh air, expressing joy at the summer, the sorghum, the cool water and the bucket of beer, the simple things we cannot take for granted. Ali Akkour (trans. Alaa Alqaisi) reads the land as a body through mythology, describing its sinews of Sisyphus. Subhro Bandopadhyay (trans. Sampurna Chattarji) gives us language as a systolic/diastolic beat, and evokes a snake that swallows up villages and language itself, enabled by the inaction of a people accustomed to greed and lethargy.

This issue also features a selection of Hungarian women poets (trans. Erika Mihálycsa and Ottilie Mulzet), writing from the wreckage of post-WWII Hungary, and the Stephen Spender Prize-winning poem, 2024 by Laoighseach Ní Choistealbha, translated by Ellen Corbett, with a medical view of the woman's body that brings the darkness of its history to light. I am grateful for these poems that give a density and language and depth of description to such experiences, and the skeletons in the closet of the 20th century.

As I worked on this issue, I also translated Gabriela Mistral's classic book of poems, *Desolación*, into English, to accompany events surrounding the 80th anniversary of her Nobel Prize in Chile. Mistral has a very particular relation to the land and to rhythm, which she developed through her verse, her studies of nature (she wrote letters to forest engineers and scientists asking about the properties of plants and metals), her friendships, and her readings of theosophy. I am particularly fond of her book *Tala*, whose name in Spanish comes from the word talar, which refers to cutting down trees, but which also suggests the rhythmic cycle in classical music and philosophy from India, a tradition known to Mistral. 'Desolación' is and is not 'Desolation'. The translation was not an easy task, and I do not consider this version to be definitive; the book is larger than one remembers, with poetry about life, pain and nature, in a style that ranges from lullabies to poems in prose. I completed the work quickly to meet deadlines, but with poetry, one can revise endlessly, and the book is still being translated somewhere deep within me.

Translating is a form of active reading that feels like light passing through the stained glass of the body; to translate is to traspasar, to use a Mistralian word, with all the refractions (and actions) that might result. This work—the poet's first—is miscellaneous, as it was compiled by teachers who organized Mistral's unpublished works, but reading in retrospect, one does find patterns in Mistral's search for beauty and meaning within the 'frozen steppe' of the spirit. The desolation refers to the spiritual idea of a desert void of goodness— any divine presence—and also more literally to the harsh, solitary landscapes of Magallanes, in the icy, wind-blasted south of Chile, where Mistral wrote her poems. Her writing also incorporates the agricultural language of harvesters, sheaves, ears of grain, fields, dew, birds; and the language of contrasts, such as cold that melts into heat, or beauty that becomes an extension of ugliness (and vice versa), like a tree from its roots. The sweet surrender of the clay to the potter's hands enables its transformation. A different notion of time begins to reign.

Mistral's work can be read along with that of so many other poets who interpret the signs given to us by nature, such as Rabindranath Tagore, who appears in a series of poems in *Desolación*, and who was anthologised in Mistral's Lecturas para mujeres. No writer works alone, and editing a magazine, like translating works by writers past and present, is a way of putting collaboration into practice. In the first moments that I entered Mistral's imagination, her barren lands and her fertilities, letting her spirit flow through me and translate me, I was disturbed and moved by her romantic and brutal images of death and childhood, her idea of a beauty that exists within and beyond the human flesh. But ultimately, I found joy in the work, and it was also with joy that I worked on this issue, with its thoughtful cover by Chilean artist Estéfani Díaz, who works with Mistralian influences. Her images, cyanotypes with blue leaves, evoke for me the sea at the heart of the desert.

My deep gratitude to Janani Ambikapathy for trusting me as guest editor, to the excellent MPT team for their affection and support, and to the poets, translators and readers of this issue, a source of hope in our collective work to care for literature and this blue planet.

Artist's Note: Estéfani Díaz Azúa

Thinking about the rhythms of the land inevitably leads me to the desert, and to the beings that dwell there, even if they are hidden by the word. The landscapes here—the cover and the three inside images—are cyanotypes that I composed starting from the image of the flowering desert, working with the veins of leaves and plants gathered in different parts of Chile. They attempt to transmit the fertile, throbbing pulse of the womb that sustains life, just as the skeleton sustains the body.

ESTÉFANI DÍAZ AZÚA is a cultural mediator, oral narrator and Spanish language teacher with a diploma in Children's and Young Adult Literature. She is an activist focused on promoting childhood education and the flowering of affect, a lesbian mother, and a constant apprentice of graphic arts that extend the languages of the word and the symbolic universe.

SELECTION OF HUNGARIAN WOMEN POETS

Translated from Hungarian by Erika Mihálycsa
and Ottilie Mulzet

Under a Pannonian Sky, an anthology of ten Hungarian women poets to
be published in the autumn of 2025 by Seagull Books, is a project that I
have been working on for a number of years. Originally, I was inspired by
an anthology of Hungarian women poets—to the best of my knowledge,
the only one published in Hungarian to date—which appeared in 1997,
featuring well over 100 poets writing from the 16th century up till the
end of the second millennium.[1] My anthology is necessarily much less
ambitious in scope, presenting a select group of ten women active
during the second half of the 20th century and into the present. Their
dates of birth span a precise half-century, from 1922 to 1972.

Like any anthology, its origins are highly subjective, even if certain
continuities of style or theme become evident. The names of some of
the poets, such as Ágnes Nemes Nagy (not featured in this selection) or
Zsuzsa Rakovszky, will no doubt be known to some readers, thanks to
the efforts of translators such as George Szirtes. Others, such as Gizella
Hervay or Magda Székely, may be less familiar.

One major common link among these women poets is their con-
nection to the intellectual and spiritual lineage of the highly influential
postwar literary journal *Újhold* (New Moon, published 1946–1948), a
cohort that emerged in the wreckage—as much moral as physical—of
post-WWII Hungary. The *Újhold* authors included an impressive
number of the authors who emerged as the leading creative personalities
of the age. An insistence on witness, on writing through difficult times,
often under the shadow of tumultuous, indeed brutally destructive,
historical events, is one of the hallmarks of the legacies of *Újhold*. These
poets present a specific variation on this legacy, creating a literature that
deserves as much attention as the canonised great names.

---

1. *Magyar költőnők antológiája* ('Anthology of Hungarian Women Poets')
Margit S. Sárdi, László Tóth (eds.), (Budapest: Enciklopédia Kiadó, 1997).

ZSUZSA RAKOVSZKY (1950–)

Face
Rembrandt, 'Portrait of Aechje Claedr'

I know that face from somewhere:
one hundred years ago, or this afternoon,
I saw her picking apples at the market
in sparse autumn light, cat underfoot,
the two vertical pleats engraved above

her nose, chiselled by a whole life's
worry and cares: behind her startled old eyes,
all of that life's light and shadow:
cooking, wash days, ill-intentioned folk,
meagre harvests, infants with running bowels,

tranquil Sundays spent with the tapestry needle,
kittens in buckets of water drowned,
the May altar decorations for the Blessed Mother,
winds blowing, hail falling, heat, light, and frost,
children departing for distant shores.

The white capelet, the bonnet with its veil —
This is a face that was never young.
It cannot be tied to any place or time,
when I was two years old, she held my hand.
Time makes other faces resemble itself,

and they too leave their handprints upon time.
There are those who polish their existence only once:
poets, popes, soldiers and kings
held up as an emblem for some city or land
while they themselves, as statues, keep existing,

their footprints remaining in the dust of that age...
But she comes to us in somewhat different guise,
not clinging to one land or century,
she has no immortal self engraved in stone,
falling apart, then reassembled, a dark river's spume.

Translated by Ottilie Mulzet

GIZELLA HERVAY (1934–1982)

A beginner at death among you
with hole-pierced forehead
bared hands
I step backward among you
my coat in the wind turned
inside out

balancing with umbrella
on time's tautened rope
bowing over the fallen
with orphan hope

bread and knife they seized
departing on luxury trains
we stay behind with our bare bones
eternal earth-dwellers

Translated by Erika Mihálycsa

ZSUZSA BENEY (1930–2006)

from *Orpheus and Eurydice (2003)*

'Our grove has withered', the trees rustling
within us, the birds, morning, and twilight.
God is dying within us.

> Accept creation from the one
> you have created. Allow the non-created
> nothing-wind to traverse your bones.

◆

As into water splashing in the depths
of wells, we dip our buckets into
the evenings of our childhood.

> No trace remains of living material.
> The soul mixes into the air.
> Falling star-love flickers out.

◆

Memory vanishes, there only remains
a crimson light reflected on the window.
Not existence, but its mirror image.

The wound of the last word, broken off,
bleeds for a long time. It is overgrown by final silence
only slowly.

◆

The rose, then its wilted stalk, then
its memory, then not even that. The infinite
cathedral of existence is oblivion.

Translated by Ottilie Mulzet

MAGDA SZÉKELY (1936–2007)

The Place

Instead of so many kinds of vanishing
possibilities
to reach that one time
that one place

To finally reach that place
where one is called
where—incomprehensibly
where—happily

Translated by Ottilie Mulzet

LAOIGHSEACH NÍ CHOISTEALBHA

Translated from Irish by Ellen Corbett

Stephen Spender prize winning poem

If I were to recommend only one poem to a first-time reader of
Ní Choistealbha, it would probably be this one. 'Scrúdú' ('Exam')
exemplifies Ní Choistealbha's oeuvre, capturing the experiences of a
young woman living in 21st-century Ireland, and projects it through the
ancient; in this case, the neolithic tombs at Newgrange
in County Meath, Ireland.

For me, too, this translation felt like a culmination; drawing on my
education in translation, my capabilities as a researcher, and my own
personal life. For the first time, the act of translation did not feel like
a game of telephone, but rather as though my own life was bleeding
over into the work. And I relished the opportunity to translate it.

That being said, this was perhaps the most *disloyal* I have ever been
in translating. I always try and stay as close to the original as possible,
but I felt the pull of an English translation, that although it was not
always one-for-one, retained the emotion and mood of the poem,
especially in dealing with such a sensitive subject matter. Imagery that
I could not convincingly put where it was originally found can be seen
later in the poem; I italicised '*adjusts*' in the third stanza, calling to
mind the pleasantries used by medical professionals at this kind of
appointment; and the final stanza is subdivided and directed at the
reader, creating a stereophonic image of both the tomb and the speaker.

Lastly, I must admit that I was very hesitant to include this
translation in my submission, considering the subject matter discussed
is still cloaked in euphemism and mentioned only in hushed tones.
But it is for these same reasons that I decided to include it, in the
hope it will raise some discussion if not also a few eyebrows.

Exam

Like any good archaeologist worth her salt,
rummaging around
in some cave or passage tomb,
my nurse dons a mask and headlamp,

and it's only now that I remember
the tufts I didn't trim,
sprouting copper under the spotlight,
like filigree across my skin,
or like the chiselled triskeles
on the entrance stone
at Newgrange.

She *adjusts* me with a lever,
peers in,
through the aperture,
to the chamber,
this dark part
that I won't ever get to see.

But after this winter solstice,
I'm as white as the paper she draped me in.
Beads of sweat gild my forehead,
nausea rises from the pit in my stomach.

I curl up on the table.
Sun-scorched,
and plead
for the darkness to return,
and for that cool shroud of ignorance,
to be replaced.

Please.
Cover me up with moss,
put back the dust
and debris,
and let me go unexamined again.

Rhythms of the Land
Focus on the Poetry of Nature

CINDY A. VELASQUEZ

Translated from Cebuano Binisaya
by Alton Melvar M. Dapanas

In *Arte de la Lengua Zebuana* ('Art of the Cebuano Language'), the
18th-century Spanish Augustinian friar Francisco Encina called the
balak—Cebuano Binisaya formal poetry—'very discreet and
enigmatic', with metaphor and mystery as its core. Encina also
admired the precolonial Cebuano speakers for mastering 'excellent
genres of verse'. Marjorie Evasco further traces the evolution of this
poetic form from Fernando Buyser's 'musically and intellectually
challenging' sonanoy (which adapted the Anglo-Italian sonnet) to
Diosdado Alesna's siniloy—characterised by rich alliteration, end
rhymes and assonance, imbuing the poem with what Evasco terms
'musical muscle' and what Resil B. Mojares described as 'mellifluity
of sound and felicitous turns of phrases'.

According to Erlinda Kintanar-Alburo, the balak, like much of
Philippine literature, draws from the rich tradition of oral storytelling
and native aesthetics. It thrives on fluid boundaries, a love for
ornamentation, and a sense of spontaneity that mirrors originality. In
its verbal form, there's often a preference for subtlety and indirection.
By the post-1970s, a new generation of Cebuano poets began to
reshape the landscape of Philippine poetry. Writing in the mother
tongue of a quarter of the country's population, they embraced free
verse and infused their work with elements that celebrated orality,
wit, social commentary, and irreverence, as noted by Mojares.

Among these voices is Dr Cindy A. Velasquez, an award-winning
songwriter, spoken word artist, and academic, whose work is deeply
grounded in the feminist poetics of the balak. Yet her debut poetry
collection *Lawas* ('Body'), published in 2016, stands in stark contrast
to the work of her contemporaries, especially those within the balak's
feminist poetics. It resists the popular trends of Instagram poetry or

the 'hugot' (hyper-cathartic) culture dominating the local spoken word scene. Instead, Velasquez's poetry is imbued with Oliverian lucidity. The islands and coastlines she writes of are places both unknown and intimately familiar. And there is Dong—an ever-present, almost spectral figure, addressed as an apostrophe, whom the poetic persona, Day or Inday, continually longs for.

Translating Velasquez is to give voice to a solivagant, navigating through a landscape of bodies—those of water and women. Her poetry weaves a narrative of love – romantic, familial, and platonic— evoking the oceanic and the sea poetry in a tradition spanning from Homer to Whitman and even Derek Walcott. To me, her work also recalls the tender eroticism of Syria's national poet Nizar Qabbani, the meditative ease of Brazilian neosymbolist Cecília Meireles and the hydropoetic enigma of T'ang dynasty Taoist elegist Ts'ao T'ang. Velasquez, however, does not align herself with these male-dominated, often Western traditions; instead, her writing stands apart: a tender exploration of her own island, her own voice.

Chicken: three tales

for the farm kids of North Cotabato

I

I have not forgotten the chicken,
its neck severed on the day of my birth.

Though it was unripe in my child's eyes,
I cannot unsee it, cannot forget it, every time
Mama performs this ritual in the kitchen.

II

On Mount Lantoy in Argao, the chickens
were laid before mountain goddess
Maria Cacao's husband: Mangao,
an offering to him for the harvest soon to come.

III

In Kidapawan, too, the chickens
were prepared: Upaw and Bugnoy.

The clouds quaked, the seconds grew thin,
the wind shivered. The earth seemed
to tighten. The flag disappeared, swallowed
by a sky made small.

Now, the owner of the worn slippers
and borrowed carabao is no longer alive.
His tattered clothes have become
his coffin and soil. The newsprint ink
now smears his hands, his forehead.
The tears of his wife fall, carving rivers
down cheeks, over her mouth, onto quivering hands.
They wander aimlessly, like the lost,
searching for corners that do not exist,
except in the fold of a newspaper.

I have not forgotten that cross drawn upon
my forehead, traced with the blood of a chicken.

No, I have not forgotten it, not even now.

When you learn of your husband's affair

Don't come home just yet. Go to the place where you first met. If the crowd grows too thick, don't cry, not yet. In the blink of an eye, the earth will tremble and turn pale. Water will surge from the deep. Now, this place is an ocean. Everything will sway with the waves. People will take the form of red mullets, octopuses, gobies, pufferfish, krill and sharks. Do not fear. Your pain will become the very air you breathe as you swim through. You are one with the ocean now. Do not hide. Everyone here is your friend. Cry, let it all spill. No one will see your tears. The water will claim them anyway. When the salt stings your eyes, tell the fish what you've seen. Let the water carry you back to the years between your embrace and the tighter embrace of the woman who holds him now. Don't ask why, don't ask when. Don't search for her name, don't look for his reasons. Swim, just swim. And then, at last, your mother will hold you, return you for a moment to the warmth of her womb.

Waiting

Once, I cooked for seven people. But now,
alone, cooking for one feels like an aching ritual:
me and my shadow both famished.

No more clatter in the kitchen.
No more crumbs to gather from the woodgrain's edge.
No more plates stacked like stories we shared.
No more praise for the stew I simmered in the quiet hours.
No more laughter caught mid-breath, no more smiles.

So tonight, I'll cook a feast of your favorites.
Seven plates with lots of adobo. We'll sit
beneath the ghosts of santol and star apple trees.
I will wait for all of you as once you have waited for me,
back when my heart was split between Hong Kong's cold streets
and the warmth of our home.

Because even the trees are long gone, swept away
by the fiercest storm to ever rage across this land.

CLAUDIA MAGLIANO

Translated from Uruguayan Spanish
by Jesse Lee Kercheval and Jeannine Marie Pitas

These six poems from *Res* ('Cow') present a darker side of human interaction with nature. They captured our attention due to its focus on the harsh realities of rural life in Uruguay. Half of Uruguay's three million people live in small cities or rural areas; beef production is a major part of the economy, and meat is a staple of the Uruguayan diet. However, a burgeoning animal rights movement is questioning the norms and customs of meat production.

Born and raised in Montevideo, Magliano did not spend time in rural areas until her thirties, when she began a romantic relationship with someone from the countryside. Until that point, she had always carried an idealised image of rural life; she was surprised to see the cruelty inherent to farming and ranching, caring for animals only to lead them to slaughter. She also noted the inherent patriarchal structures in meat production. Her goal with this book is to suggest the cruel side of rural life, which had a huge impact on her life and perspective, causing her to think in a new way about the beef she was so used to buying at the supermarket.

This conflation of violence against animals and violence against women is particularly impactful for the two of us as readers, and we are eager to share it with an English-speaking audience.

Cow

The mud destroys the meadow and it's not possible to reach the nearest town / it's 50 kilometers away it's too far to walk to / on dew-damp knees / and the vehicle blocked mud inside mud outside from the body of the farmhand and the woman waiting in the immense night / there's no moon tonight no light and the girl is braver than her mother / courageous said her grandfather and yes some good has come from this one who doesn't know her times tables but how the little one saddles up and takes off galloping / it's the brown tips of her hair in the wind scattered among the trees / surely she's well fed this pitcher I mean what a girl this little one has become, someone has to say it. Today she drank all the soup.

◆

The direction of the wind indicates surely it will rain tomorrow we'll have to shelter at home motionless our eyes glued to the window watching the raindrops / how slippery winter is and here inside there's nothing to do nothing in the country but go out across the fields one two three there are four hundred sheep with their backs painted blue the water doesn't discolor their brands even so we know very well which ones will die / now we need to separate the lambs take them from their mothers / and the dogs behind hunt for any remains that might be left. There's no soup today.

◆

To hide the glasses / cover them / the girl comes to look she wants a game something more than grass and grapefruits / picking flowers gets boring / the landscape gets boring this little one who rode the mare bareback and melted into the woods with her mother looking for who knows what / and the glasses covered on the table / it's night yes night is beginning and it's long in the country nights in the country are long they start early and don't end. She'll have to count blue sheep.

◆

To separate sheep / to close the gates so they face each other while the girl cries out one's escaping / to mount the horse to reach her surround her by force / before she dies she doesn't say bah she tries to escape / this one turned out a rebel she was born that way sheep cause trouble at times / hurry up the horse the mare whichever get on it hurry up / the eyes of the sheep are rounder now that lassoed to the hero she's going back to the slaughterhouse.

◆

There are cows that look like skeletons not because they're skinny / no / they're big like the others and look like skeletons black and white faces they look like the dead bringing threats in the night / they look like skulls their faces are scary if they look straight ahead and they look straight ahead the lights of the vehicle not the one stuck in the mud on the knees of the farmhand who dragged himself back to the village to beg for help and it was nighttime and everyone in the village was sleeping they all sleep at set hours and the lone man and his wife and girl behind him there in the distance waiting staring straight ahead at the cows that look like skeletons and are about to die just like the blue sheep.

◆

The men butcher animals because they're rough they're macho they're harsh in their task of killing animals they're not scared the men the animals are just prey and it's their destiny to be killed and the women in the kitchen are waiting for moist warm bloody meat that the men carry on their shoulders for breakfast / the women say nothing just like the animals as they're killed they say nothing / there are no traces of struggle in the deaths of the cows and the sheep / there are no traces of flight / that is their destiny to be livestock profit food for other beasts less sublime than they.

DALIA TAHA

Translated from Arabic by Sara Elkamel

Dalia Taha's most recent poetry collection, *Enter World* (forthcoming from Graywolf in my English translation in 2026), engages with the still unfolding war in Gaza. In precise, unembellished language, Taha converses with fundamentally human concepts through the lens of war—among them silence, grief, unbridled love and natural phenomena. These two poems, 'Enter Palestinian Love' and 'Enter Shadows of Trees', insist on tenderness amid violence, on finding beauty in what remains, and meaning in what is erased. Translating Taha's work has been an effort to carry over the quiet power of her voice—a voice that, through the smallest gestures, insists on the persistence of poetry even in the most desolate of times.

Enter Shadows of Trees

At Birzeit University, near the Faculty of Arts,
is a sidewalk painted white,
surrounded by four trees.

Their shadows interlace over its surface in the fall, and sparkle;
I walk after class
across light and darkness.

I cannot begin to describe the scene—
yellow, silver, green, and black.
Believe me when I say
all of it sparkles.

If you visit our school
looking for truth or questions,
for the Faculty of Sciences or Philosophy,
walk past the trees
and try—
try
to enter the world once more
through the most desolate road.

Watch how,
each day,
the wind erases another one of the trees' answers.

Enter Palestinian Love

We Palestinians
love what we love
a little more than we should.

Look how we love our universities,
our plums, our country's crisp air,
our Za'atar, our poets,
our villages blown to pieces.

We are always prepared to love
a little more than we should;
always prepared to die
a little more than we should.

KENZABURŌ ŌE

Translated from Japanese by Akagi Kobayashi

Kenzaburō Ōe, who won the prestigious Akutagawa Prize in 1958 when only 23 years old, and later the Nobel Literature Prize in 1994, drew on the deep stresses of a society forced to make a sudden and drastic change from a totalitarian to a democratic order, as a result of defeat in war. He expressed a cry for human dignity, examined against the pull and friction of social 'progress' in his *Hiroshima Notes*.

Many of his later novels contained a retelling of his personal life, as he continued to explore the question of life and connections with time and place. He returned frequently physically and emotionally to the environment that gave birth to him, the deep forests of Shikoku. In *Under My Own Tree* (2001) he narrates the mystery of rebirth—that he may die but would be given another birth—as told by his mother, which left a deep impression on him, and remained at the core of his being and relationship to the world.

Politically, Ōe became an active pacifist and environmentalist. The nuclear fallout from the Great East Japan Earthquake (11 March, 2011) disturbed him greatly, after which he dedicated even more time and energy campaigning against the use of nuclear power. 'Memento Poem' ('Katami-no-uta') was thought to be from that period, but it was in fact a commissioned work from 2006, which was published later as a postscript to *In Late Style*, his last work, in 2013. He was 70 when he wrote this to be left in memory of his life, but ten years later, he noted that it was like a 'letter to himself at 80', having survived events such as 3/11, as foretold in the poem.

I have been fascinated by the consistent expressions of his identity that had deep roots in the way of life borne out of the natural environment of his ancestral village. His lasting belief in humanity and his life as a peace and environmental activist came out of the wisdom of earth, passed down to him in the guise of a myth, which forms the backbone of 'Memento Poem'.

I first saw Ōe on TV, in a series of discussions with teenagers on topics such as 'Why do we have to go to school?'. I was impressed to see this elderly and respected author attempting to engage in frank exchanges with youngsters. I am sure that he was working from his earlier experience and struggle, to help the new generation. In some of his early work, Ōe describes a sense of betrayal against the adult world that superficially accepted change while resisting genuine transformation.

Ōe died aged 88 on 3 March, 2023.

Memento Poem

The little thing that has overcome
the inherent violence of birth
keeps shut its yet unseeing eyes tight.
My first grandchild—
I see my likeness in his face,
and as I draw closer,
sensing the movement of my face,
the little thing starts to cry . . .
Is this not my own old self,
screaming and crying
in the guise of an infant?
The years and months that this child will live
will surely exceed the cruelty of seventy years of my life.
The little thing
has no words yet to ask a question
but spreads its precise miniature fingers
to grope the air incessantly.

In the wooded hills of Shikoku,
A legend is told of 'One's Own Tree'.
Those who live and die in the valley
each have their own tree.
When a man or a woman dies,
the soul rises to the upper reaches
and settles at the root of their Own Tree.
In time, the soul descends into the valley
and enters the breast of a baby about to be born.
If a child wishes fervently
at the foot of his Own Tree,

his same self, but much aged
will (or may) come to meet him.

Until I was ten years old,
everything and everyone in the country was embroiled in war.
We children sang the words —
We will not regret could we but die by the side of our Lord the Emperor.
The day our Lord
with the voice of a human being
announced that the country was defeated in war,
the head master stood up, faced the radio and shouted.
It is not possible for us to live our lives again!
Silence echoed against the clear blue sky.

I went into the woods and running through the mixed forest of cedars
    and cypresses,
reached the sun-lit grove of broadleaved trees.
Amidst them stood the group of tall fir trees
which were our Own Trees of all of our clan.
I waited at the foot of one of the younger trees
wishing to meet my aged self
and ask him . . .
Will I be able to live my life again?
As dusk descended on the woods
the sudden noise of foot steps
threw me into a frenzy of fear.
With my hair standing on end
I ran into the slope of Nikko firs
rolled head-over-heels and slid downhill.

My whole body was covered in cuts and grazes
and my mother, stripping me naked,
applying tinctures of herbs she had gathered herself,
bemoaned.
How could anyone say,
in a place where children were listening,
that we could not live our lives again?
And my mother continued with the words
that were to remain a mystery for a long time —
I am not able to live my life again. But
we are.

A compatriot and friend, robbed of his country,
who shared the sense of uncertainty with me and struggled,
who was also fighting leukemia,
adopted in his final years as the theme of his study
expressions and a style of living
chosen by artists of a certain type, facing imminent death,
whose lives would not reach gentle maturity.
They deny tradition and refuse to harmonize with society,
and steadfast within negativity,
stand perpendicularly and alone. And
some achieve uniqueness of creativity hitherto unknown . . .
The final fax from his deathbed in New York —
Do not fear the contradiction that tears through your inner being in
    old age,
gauge what challenges lie, and stretch
your arms out beyond them,
from your unstable foothold.

Suddenly I find myself
entrenched in the predicament of old age,
stubborn and isolated.
I find closeness only with emotions of negativity.
There is nothing strange in denouncing the machinery of world
    destruction
that my century has amassed,
but my doubts also extend to
most attempts towards their demolition.
I curl up crouched on shaky ground, asking
what little worth did my creative work ever have?

The old man who kept me waiting that day,
at the foot of my Own Tree,
was no other than my present self
. . . yet to find the words to reply to the young boy.

My grandchild, after a year since his birth,
shows not even the slightest trace of resemblance of old age
which I am sure I glimpsed.
He stares back at me,
his skin taut and glowing.
By his side, crouching low
is my predicament of old age
which cannot be knocked down
or overcome,
but can be deepened.
That is what my friend wrote, in his unfinished book.
So, then, if I deepen
the emotion of negativity of old age
and stretch out my hands

from uncertain grounds to reach the heights,
is it possible that they may perhaps touch some thing or being?
Establishing negativity has always been
not only a denial of half-hearted hope
but also a denial of agreement with any despair. . .
The one year old innocent, here beside me,
is new to everything,
he is exploring the unknown avidly.

Inside me, for the first time,
my mother's words shed their mystery.
The old man will reply to the little ones.
I cannot live my life again, but
we can live our lives again.

MAARJA PÄRTNA

Translated from Estonian by Hilary Bird

The work of Estonian poet Maarja Pärtna combines historical recall of trauma—Estonia experienced three wars, three revolutions and four occupations during the 20th century—with worry about climate change, articulating a growing sense of danger from destruction of the environment and loss of biodiversity. Her poems are in direct dialogue with the natural world, how it smells, how it feels, how it looks, its textures and rhythms, its diversity and its fate.

This poetry combines a gentle sensual experience of the world with deep concern about its future. Issues explored include the interaction of humans with animals and plants, the importance of friendship, kindness and empathy, the need for a rejection of war and violence and resistance to environmental hooliganism. A feeling of organic growth is endemic: subjective experiences generate abstract thoughts and large-scale generalisations start from little things.

The six poems here are unpublished in English translation. They are taken from the collection *On the Eve of Insurrection* ('Ülestõusmise Serval', 2024). The first poems in the book focus on experiences in a small shared garden, amid flowers, herbs and pots; as the collection progresses, with war planes flying overhead and the thermometer registering the hottest temperatures ever, the poems extol, amid anxiety, the comforts of literature, of friendship and for the hope for a better world through empathy and cooperation.

The end of the Holocene age need not be the end of the world . . .

... old, difficult pain is all around us, everywhere.

Epp Annus

from *Ühisaias* ('In the shared garden')
Pelgupaik ('The refuge')

Smells of soil and fresh grass after rain
lemon balm, yarrow and chamomile.
I breathe the breath of plants,
I hide my face in almond meadowsweet.
Everything seems the same as usual,
the sun rises and sets, doors open and close,
but cracks appear in people,
they split like unfired clay amphorae
and collapse silently in upon themselves.
An old, heavy pain seeps from the shards,
fear of war, detachment, depression.
I know that the meadowsweet smell that fills the honeycomb pots
of my heart is not meant for me, but I can enjoy it —
that's why a world of the senses is
my unwavering and only refuge.

Varemerohi ('Comfrey')

The bee drowns blissfully in the pollen in the pot, sacrificing itself.
I stand on the edge of the garden of earthly delights
and caress coarse ruined greenery with my fingers;
the wide leaves in my palm, wisely, do not share
the secret of their nature.
Every hot summer the bones-shards of charred forests
chronicle a changing world
ever more clearly than before. Humans too
drown in words like the bee in honey,
when they forget the language of the Earth.

Rohukõrred ('Blades of grass')

I breathe the scent of fresh mint.
Young, green shoots explode
from my breaking breast, and I turn totally green.
I cultivate a wilder lust-for-life-garden, I bolster my friends with words,
I am solid ground in a stormy wind.
A warplane flies over us with a sulphureous roar.
Blades of grass rustle in the wind, complex, defensive
co-operation. If it's true that evil eviscerates,
that every tiny cruelty mirrors great violence,
goodness must be like this too. The more the danger,
the greater weight of every little act of kindness.

ELENA SALAMANCA

Translated from Salvadoran Spanish by Ryan Greene

In the poem '*Sin más que mis uñas, en algunos sueños, yo también
he rascado la tierra*' ('With nothing but my nails, in some dreams,
I too have scratched the earth'), Salamanca links her experience of
uterine myomatosis, endometriosis, and a subsequent hysterectomy
to her great-great grandmother's experience of losing her newborns to
neonatal tetanus in a town at the foot of the Izalco volcano.

As a translator, I'm drawn to the multidisciplinary quality of
Salamanca's work, and I'm moved by the ways her poetry models
the power and possibility of embodied, ecological approaches to
documentation, witness and imagination. This is the joy of reading
a historian's poetry and a poet's history.

This poem in particular serves as the coda to Salamanca's
collection *TEPHRA (Three Ashes)* which is the second book in her
ecopoetic trilogy, *TENTACLE AND VELVET*. Across the trilogy,
Salamanca roots herself in an exploration of connections between
personal and political memory, the natural world, and the history of
El Salvador, ranging from pre-history through the civil war (1980–1992)
to the present and beyond. She has stated that her goal in the project
is to 'write a history of significant otherness [borrowing Donna
Haraway's term]: flora, fauna, and the more-than-human relationships
that we (women) establish with them.'

Throughout, she interweaves understandings of nature, geology,
climate change, and gender to develop a poetic trilogy in which, as she
puts it, 'the history of women, the history of volcanoes, oral history,
and scientific studies frame an alternative history of El Salvador.'

Author's Note

This selection from *TEPHRA (Three Ashes)* includes 'With nothing but my nails, in some dreams, I too have scratched the earth', the collection's coda.

In the coda, Toribia is my great-great-grandmother, Toribia Mancía (1873–1936), the mother of my great-grandmother, María del Carmen Evarista Mancía Rojas (1904–1992). Both lived in the pueblo of Asunción de Izalco, a significant space in the uprising and the subsequent massacre in 1932. After reviewing the records of births and deaths at the church of Dolores de Izalco, I could reconstruct and weave a biography of my great-great-grandmother, who had only two surviving children out of her eight births. María (my great-grandmother) was her firstborn.

My great-great-grandmother gave birth eight times and of those births, four children died of 'alferecía', as neonatal tetanus was called at the start of the century. These deaths coincided with the studies of tetanus, the experimentation and creation of the vaccine. Neonatal tetanus caused seizures and fever until the little ones died. In some regions it was called the 'seven-day sickness', since that was the period of incubation and death. Sure enough, my great-great-grandmother's babies died between five and seven days after their birth. The coda was written days before my total hysterectomy operation in 2023, in which I lost my uterus due to the growth of 36 tumors or giant myomas.

Writing about illness, writing about trauma and writing about landscape are, for me, one and the same in this book, divided into diverse temporal strata and our relations with other non-human creatures, especially female mammals, birds and flowers, who have suffered environmental crises, social injustice and our own human violence.

With nothing but my nails, in some dreams,
I too have scratched the earth

[coda]

I

The Cenzontle
starts singing at four in the morning
as I
tossing and turning with fever
wonder:
why didn't I inherit a diamond ring.

Not a farm nor a hectare,
Not even a house.
A ring,
an obscene stone,
the size of an ice cube.

A cocktail ring,
like in the dry-law days
to say somehow that I was worth it
like those women who slipped out alone
on the sly
in the middle of the night.

That I've been worth it because
it's been years
decades

a century
and that stone
hasn't broken.
Nor like a river rock,
between so many bodies and so many hands,
has it ended up with some fissure.
Nor with the blows of tragedy
nor with the hands digging in the dirt
has it lost its shine.

Something:
a ring
to sell at Monte de Piedad
before dawn
with nobody to see me lining up
to pawn whatever it is:
The past.
The debts.
The lineage.
It makes no difference:
it's all the same.
The bird is generous and sings
as I keep plotting with my own shadow:
What did Toribia do
during her eighth birth.

Golden hour starts before
five in the morning.
No one's sure exactly when it begins,
perhaps just the birds,
but it gleams

and there's a confusion:
it looks just like the sunset from the wrong side of the world.

I take advantage of the confusion and draw my body on the wall
next to the bed
with my shadows.

My grandmother taught me to play with shadows
during the nights of war at the end of the century.
It was the 20th century,
but it seemed more like
the time of ancient wars.
Every war is in some way the same:
thousands of unknown dead
and illuminations with candles,
perhaps
robbed from the churches
in those strange lootings
where the bread
the wine
the altars' lace
and the virgins' gold were left in place.
But not the candles,
the wax,
the matches,
the pieces of ocote . . .
What shines in another way
was more sacred.
What did Toribia do with the dead child

and the umbilical cord infested with tetanus.
What did she do to not die.

Because she didn't die.

She simply did what she always did
when her children died on her:
a small burial
next to the church
or at the edge of a milpa.

Under a dry tree
burying umbilici rotten
with tetanus.
The tetanus toxoid was first used in 1924,
by then Toribia had given birth to all her children.
And in Toribia's town,
past Izalco de Dolores, everything arrived late.
The civil registry, love letters, science.
Everything, except the volcano's ash.
In 1924,
when the tetanus toxoid was used as a vaccine,
Toribia had already given birth to all her children.
Six dead,
two alive.
And she was left dry and forgotten in the strongest years of her youth.

What did Toribia do,
I sometimes wonder,
during her eighth birth,
with the sixth dead child.

With a fever
she herself also infected with tetanus in the umbilicus,
where,
supposedly,
life began.

Neither delirious nor in transit,
simply kneeling in the field
opening holes in the dirt
with just her nails.
She didn't wear rings, Toribia,
just black nails,
half-moons of deep black dirt,
volcanic,
good for planting, they'd say now in the nurseries.
Dark thick layer
atop ancient ashes, porous rocks
dragged by the oceans' poundings,
rocks which once were under the open sea
and now form sediments of time.

What did you do when you had a fever, Toribia.
What did you do after the last birth.
After the last dead child,
what did you do to not die?

II

What did you do to not kill yourself?

III

With no tool but my nails
in some dreams
I too have scratched the dirt.
And where I feared I would find cadavers,
I found roots.
Short roots, small connections
long roots that stretch under houses and other trees
and interweave, like Toribia's umbilical cord must connect,
with other palpitating spaces:
burrows
where other mammals give birth to their tiny little creatures.
Long embryonic extensions that snaked with an undular motion
not of tremor nor chaos,
of life.

Perhaps between these roots,
in unknown vegetal spaces,
Toribia buried the umbilici
like the tradition of births dictated.

But all women plant the umbilicus like a seed.
Life.
That which is covered so it might germinate,
because what pulses is celebrated,
not what's infected
and stiff.

In those dreams,
I've found those umbilici,

fertilized amid the shards
of the deciduous tree
which knows that
one must detach to bloom again.

Perhaps
those cursed umbilici on the earth
managed to germinate in the depths
according to an organic justice
exerted by the centuries.
I don't dictate it,
it's been dictated by the Earth.

IV

Open seas I trace with the body's contour
under the sheets
rise up from the motion of the fever and its deliria.
It's not the ocean,
it's the sweat of a sick woman
who wakes at dawn
pierced by ancient errors.

Sea-body between sheets embroidered
exquisitely
with erroneous initials.
Like anyone who's born and is swaddled in trousseau,
ménage,
lineage.

To live as though fumbling with your hands in antique sheets
and embroidered tatted tablecloths
laid out for banquets which no one will attend.
Lace woven with cold needles,
like that needle which seemed to be God's eye,
a ship,
or a knife.
Lace of blind knots,
as my great-grandmother called
those which can't
be untied.

That knot which is only untied
by breaking it
like an infected umbilical cord
before the tetanus vaccine existed.

V

I go back to my mother's house
on the verge of breaking genealogy.
My body will be left split in two,
by the systems,
I'll lose the connections to the organs that,
in school diagrams,
look like flowers.
Neither the umbilical cords that tempt with strangling yourself
before birth
nor the confines of hormonal shifts
will be able to save me.

Always dreaming of forests,
always behind Toribia,
unable to reach even her shadow with my hand,
my body became fruit.
Inverted flower.
Like a fig.
The wasp enters and dies
and that death is transformed into something else.
The fig tree always blooms
but nobody notices.
Because it blooms within.

HÅKAN SANDELL

Translated from Swedish by Bill Coyle

Håkan Sandell is one of the most important poets writing in Swedish today. I have long experience translating Sandell; I received an NEA grant in 2011 to complete a manuscript of his work, later published by Carcanet under the title *Dog Star Notations: Selected Poems 1999–2016*. The translations I'm sending today are of more recent work.

The two translations presented here are of poems from Håkan Sandell's 2023 collection *Jorden öppnar portarna* ('Earth Opens Its Gates'), where they appear sequentially, 'To Our Earth' being immediately followed by 'And When Another Hymn Sounds'. The entire collection, Sandell tells me, resulted from an attempt to write more spontaneously than he had before, almost to 'channel' the poems. Not that this vatic approach precluded attention to verse technique. Quite the opposite: The vigorous accentual verse in which the poems are cast, with assonance typically taking the place of full end-rhymes, was as necessary to their composition as to their final form.

To Our Earth

Earth, earth, hurtled through space and cloud-smoke, backdropped
      by the absconding sun, you stand out
like a dark leaf or the shadow of a passing arrow, the one dark jewel
      remaining in the golden crown.
Your darkness woven together with the bleached yellow grass beneath
      increasing gusts only the lining of my coat
makes bearable, though the wreaths on graves, too, have been drained
      of their luster and ribbons as they thin and decompose.

Your rounded dirt pile into which everything at last vanishes. There,
      too, the electric cars from quiet, empty city centers
and shrinking ice sheets from collapsing mountainsides will be sifted,
      high-rises fill their own cellars.
There, among crushed teams of horses, in the *Mahabharata*, heads
      have been cloven into bloody halves
like blood-tinted pairs of earrings, sinking down into shafts towards
      unrolled lengths of shadow, now as in the remote past.

Earth, earth, with your long hair in a brown rivulet over the broad
      of your back and your wide tattooed fields,
your naked shoulder blades and the barren industries that the
      wildfires of autumn walks have already concealed.
On the outdoor seating, blankets heavy with damp lie under
      hawk-grey skies following the evening's expeditions,
an evening that, closed now, has only the starry highway binding its
      glittering darkness like a belt of great cities.

Here's Persephone, your daughter, with the lipstick kissed lightly away
   at the corners of her mouth, rain brimming her lacquer bag,
she slinks slimly, quickly, through the door of the dark, brake lights
   shining like her pomegranate in the autumn blackness.
It is I who shall be crucified for an offering over the croplands, the
   sunken apple pearled with dew be eaten from below.
My sex will be the first thing cut off, then my tongue, then the words
   will begin to glitter, dust falling over the dark loam.

And When Another Hymn Sounds

from out of the closed-off marriages,
      and softly through these cardboard-thin walls
I can hear it, albeit baffled.
      And from my own shortcomings, also.
From each thing in this sketch of an existence
      is audible a half-sung, half-spoken hymn,
the thousand causes, difficult to trace,
      whose rising music nonetheless shakes one.
From archaic birch trees with grey trunks
      like abdicated queens ready to depart.
From the wrecked and abandoned junkies
      who've turned self-destruction into an art.
The countless many of them I have seen
      with heavy sand in the folds of their knees.
Yes, all the hastily scrawled signatures
      whose meanings remain largely hidden.
I don't know what has happened with me,
      but that rat, now, there at the park's edge,

its back to me, running on stiff legs,
    having lived its three or four seasons,
seems to constitute a kind of message,
    and an almost triumphant one, vaunting
that it was here, beneath a heaven
    reflecting other heavens vaulting
through the many worlds with many mansions
    its own consciousness made manifest.
One whose death, displayed for a brief time,
    will say, I was here! this life of mine,
though short and valued at little, all the same
    rejoiced fully beneath the sky's wide grey,
and as regards my way, how I rang
    like a lead bell through the whole creation.

MARINA TSVETAEVA

Translated from Russian by Stephen Capus

Marina Tsvetaeva is one of the greatest Russian poets of the 20th century, but she is also one of the most difficult to translate. One of the reasons why Tsvetaeva's poems constitute such a challenge for the translator is that they offer, in an unusually pure and uncompromising form, an instance of poetic language as it has been defined by the 20th century Russian critic Roman Jakobson. According to Jakobson, a poem is constructed, not just through the progressive development of a linear idea—of a story, an argument or a description—but also through the elaboration of patterns based on contrast and similarity, patterns which occur at all levels of the poetic text, from semantics and syntax to sound, and which on the level of sound include rhyme and metre.

Many of Tsvetaeva's poems, including some of her most characteristic, offer remarkably little by way of progressively developed argument, narrative or description. Their 'content', in the prosaic sense of the word, can sometimes be quite negligible, to the point where her more experimental texts begin to resemble the 'zaum', or trans-sense language, practised by the Russian futurist poet Velimir Khlebnikov. But even in her more conventional poems discursive thought, unfolding along the horizontal axis of the text, intersects with complex structures of the kind described above: structures which are based on relations of similarity and contrast, and which are displayed along the vertical axis of the text.

Throughout her life Tsvetaeva contended with adversity, which only increased after she went into exile in Western Europe following the October Revolution. However, even as she became progressively more alienated from the Russian émigré community in Paris throughout the 1930s, so her sense of communion with the natural world deepened. Above all, she felt a close connection with trees,

whether the rowan trees of Moscow, the forests around Prague
or the tree which she felt to live on in the desk which accompanied
her in exile. The translations which follow attempt to reproduce
the intricate patterns of metaphorical connections through which
Tsvetaeva was able to articulate her love of nature, and which are the
source of what the critic Simon Karlinsky has described as the
'incantatory' power of her poetry.

from *Poems about Moscow*

The leaves drifted down
And the rowan tree burst
Into clusters of flame
On the day of my birth.

And everywhere church bells
Were quarrelling on
The day of the Holy
Apostle, Saint John.

And today I still hanker
To taste once again
The rowan's tart berries,
Like clusters of flame.

16 August 1916

from *Desk*

My desk, I give thanks to you
For remaining steadfast and true,
Always there to be counted upon,
Beside me wherever I've gone.

My stalwart mule of a desk,
Thank you for bearing the stress
Of the burden of dreams which I placed
On your back with unfailing grace.

Stern mirror of truth (and yet
A door which might also have led
To worldly temptation), I thank
You for always refusing point-blank

All meanness, for blocking the road
To shallow delight, saying 'no'
To resentment, an oaken weight
Resisting the madness of hate.

A plank of wood—yet alive,
I give thanks that you always thrived,
That, like me, you never once ceased
To breathe, to expand, to increase,

Till you grew so open, so wide,
That, caught in the flood, I was soaked,
Like a beach that's drenched by the tide,
As I clung to your planks of oak!

Chained to your side from first light,
I'm glad that each time I took flight,
Like a pitiless master you tracked
Me down and then dragged me back

To my chair—there's work to do still!
I thank you for curbing my will,
For setting me free from the spell
Of the world, like the wizard who tells

The sleeper to wake. Scars acquired
In battle, you turned into fire,
Into columns of words that bleed—
The living scroll of my deeds.

Like the saint on his pillar of stone,
In you I found freedom, a home,
You lit up my way like the Lord
Who once guided the Hebrew hordes.

Then forever be blessed by me,
Feel the press of my elbows and knees
As your hard oak edge, like a saw,
Cuts through my breast to its core.

July 1933

PIEDAD BONNETT

Translated from Colombian Spanish by Richard Gwyn

Although Piedad Bonnett is not renowned as a writer committed to environmental protest, I have noted a concern with the natural world as a recurrent substratum of her work: there is often, in her poetry, an awareness of ecology in its broadest sense, in the relationship between living things and their surroundings, which draws on what might be termed the collective unconscious of the world and its occupants, human and non-human.

While Bonnett's poetry often invokes themes of existential threat or imminent violence, and reflects on strains of cultural and personal anxiety, there is also a deep nostalgia for a world untrammelled by man-made or extraneous miseries, perhaps exemplified by the sea cucumber in 'Lesson in Survival', which can only find peace by disgorging its own intestines, or—perhaps more disturbingly—the universal tragedy of post-modern isolation experienced by the young man, Sun Dayong, in 'The world wide and strange', in which our access to news items of this kind is reliant on precisely the kind of electronic devices that Sun Dayong was employed in assembling, and which led directly to his suicide. In this way, we might reflect, we distance ourselves from the abundance and beauty of the world touched upon in 'Harmony', in which we can hear the lovemaking of the tigers, and relish the eternal dance of the stars.

Yet these poems are by no means simplifications of complex matters: they take their subject material seriously, and go straight to the heart of things, in language which is often simple and direct, but by no means 'easy'; and translating the apparently simple is, in its own way, as tough as translating a very complex text. Conveying the straightforward and accessible language of Bonnett's Spanish without compromising the depth of sentiment it contains (and without resorting to banalities) was one of the challenges of translating these poems.

Harmony

Listen how the tigers love each other
and the jungle fills with their deep panting,
and the night splits open with their ferocious lightning.
See how the stars revolve in harmony's
eternal dance and their silence
overflows with vegetable whispers.
Smell the thick honey the trees distill,
the dark milk their leaves exude.
The entire universe braids and unbraids
in infinite secret intercourse.
Wise geometries interlace the forms
of sweet snails and ungrateful serpents.
In the sea is a siren song.
Touch my skin,
quaking for you and exposed to thorns,
before the rhythm of my blood falls quiet,
before it returns to water and to the earth.

Like a Tree

Like a tree grateful for the rain
unfolding its branches
I was so steeped in your desire
that I blossomed into words.
Now, like a tree in winter,
naked, stripped bare,
I want to sink my roots into the earth,
drink its sap.
And be silent like a tree. To clothe myself with silence
to hear what crackles within you,
what speaks without yet speaking.

Lesson in Survival

There is nothing beautiful about the sea cucumber.
It is, in truth, an animal without grace,
like its name.
At the bottom of great oceans,
unmoving, soft, amorphous,
it remains
condemned to the sand,
set apart from the beauty that the sea displays
above its body.
It is known that
when the sea cucumber gets a whiff of death
in the predator that threatens it,
it expels
not only its intestines
but the entire cluster of its gut,
which serves as food for its enemy.
In a clean ritual
the sea cucumber flees from whatever threatens to harm it.
To survive, it stays empty.
Relieved of itself and free of others
it mutates its being.
And little by little
its innards
recompose.
And it returns to being, in salty lethargy,
an entity at peace that lives in its own way.

Bats

I thought that one great sorrow would displace
the smaller sorrows.
Nevertheless, there they are
screeching away, head under wing,
gnashing their teeth, never relinquishing
the piece of flesh to which they cling —
while I sigh,
sing myself a song,
and say I am the mother who bears them
and will have to make my instrument of bone
and of my days an impregnable wall
so that they no longer creep, nor bewilder,
and I can focus on the silence
where Sorrow incubates its great egg.

The world wide and strange

Concerning Sun Dayung, a young Chinese man.
They say that he was twenty-four,
that he assembled parts of electronic devices,
that he lived far from home, in Hon Hai,
that he worked twelve hours a day, like all his colleagues,
that he slept in his spare time, like all his colleagues,
that among them talk was scarce
because they barely knew each other.
No one knows anything else,
except that he jumped from the small window in his two metre
by two metre room,
and that he is one of many who have jumped
in the past year.
Ah, yes. The news item said another thing:
that the factory managers
have attached bars on all the windows
to avoid more suicides.
I read this item on Google, on my laptop computer,
on which I can see the whole world, wide and strange.

YAN LI

Translated from Chinese by Anna Yin

I have translated more than 50 poems by Yan Li—some from earlier years, others more recently—and each one offers its own unique blend of surprise, wisdom, and dark humour. 'Waking Water Up' revealed to me how the fate of trees mirrors our own, underscoring the urgent need for awakening. In an interview, Yan Li described himself as a pessimist about the future. Many of his poems confront war and human greed; 'The Enigma of History' stands out as a powerful example.

Waking Water Up

Every tree
holds a chance to rise beyond transcendence
If a notice from axes and chainsaws
arrives
there is no need to seek another burial ground
No matter how shattered their bodies
they will be cremated to their fullest
Humans compose music by trees' cries
dance along with their flames
then heat water to wake it from ignorance

The Enigma of History

Where have you arrived?
Electricity has been invented for over 200 years,
and the posture of looking out is far too outdated,
so you gaze downward into the world of smartphones.

I suspect, in the gaps language cannot breach,
lie untouched remnants of the cosmos—
a realm untouched by the next station of video life forms.

In any case, wherever you may arrive,
there won't be more pleasant weather,
nor will it change the naturally gifted local specialties.

Mars may hold the hope of receiving SOS calls,
but you still have to return to today's Earth,
which is fraught with crises.

Where does today fit into the enigma of history?
You and weapons climb the branches of humanity,
ready for full bloom.

EMI MIYAOKA

Translated from Japanese by the author

I believe that poetry is sometimes written in moments when one becomes a part of the great flow of the world and loses the sense of being oneself. And that is a very happy experience. The poem 'PARALLEL MOTION, FLYING CATS' SILENCE' is one of those precious works that I was able to write with the feeling of becoming a part of the world. During a period when I was on leave from work, I wrote this piece during an about 30-minute walk along the Yodo Riverbank in my hometown of Hirakata City. It was born from the feeling of being surrounded by nature and I did almost no rewriting afterward. Even now, looking back, it feels like a small miracle that emerged after the long passage of time in my life.

'PARALLEL MOTION, FLYING CATS' SILENCE' is also musical score for mixed chorus and piano, based on four poems from my first and second books, published along with the premiere in Tokyo, 2014. The suite was played by Waseda University, Kobe-U, Doshisha-U, Hokkaido-U, Mixed Chorus of Sapporo City, etc (2014–present). In Japan, I've been fortunate that many university and high school choirs, with the fresh brilliance of youth, have sung this suite. I am deeply grateful to Tetsutaro Masui, who composed such fantastical pieces, and to everyone involved.

Poetry allows each reader to bring forth their own interpretations. The author's interpretation is not necessarily the correct one; rather, infinite interpretations can coexist. That is because poetry is something that 'happens' or 'arises' in a given place and time. The flying cat that appears in this poem is an imaginary creature, but I hope for a broad-minded world where such beings might exist. Especially in today's unstable world, even if it is small and powerless, I hope this poem can bring comfort to someone, somewhere.

PARALLEL MOTION, FLYING CATS' SILENCE

In a sunset glow, flying cats are flying to—
People say flying cats go beautifully with a sunset glow,
it's something like a bright red ripe tomato and cream cheese.
Flying cats form a large group,
it looks like it is taking up the horizon.
The whole group is moving west slowly.
Group after group,
spreading all over the wide-open sky.
A situation of cats moving their four limbs in the sky,
looking exactly like a huge air corridor there.
That is eternal, as it were.

Flying cats are high-minded.
They never meow.
Silent,
it seems they accept their special existences
having forgiven themselves to melt into the great nature.
While their ecology is well investigated,
people say nothing about it.

People become silent and point to the sky,
(See, flying cats are flying to—)
look up at the sky,
and nod to themselves inside their hearts.
They are something sacred—forgiven existences,
as if the spectacle itself strongly confirms our being.

The wind blows against them.
While flying cats march out of step a little,
that doesn't influence the general situation.
The group parade is calmly going on with a powerful step.
When we look upward, there are some frolicking with each other.
The wind keeps on blowing—
For some time, we look up at the distant sky,
and our thoughts go to the far off future of the Earth
that needs the existence of living beings like, for instance, flying cats;
those are released quietly in the Galaxy.

BEGOÑA UGALDE

Translated from Chilean Spanish by Drago Yurac

Begoña Ugalde was born in Santiago, Chile, but spent her summers in Papudo, a fishing village originally inhabited by the Changos. There, she learned to ride waves and converse with the tides. She also took walks through gorges and native forests, now devastated by real estate companies that have carved through the hills, leaving tons of debris. After living in Barcelona for a few years, Ugalde decided to return to the fifth region of Chile and settle between Valparaíso and the mouth of the Aconcagua River, where species survive in a precarious balance, surrounded by oil and coal refineries.

'My heart is an active volcano' is a poem by Ugalde that deals with a journey and a transformation, while climbing a mountain in the Andes Mountains in Chile. It is a long poem that shows the strength of a body in urgency, when it connects and becomes sensitive to the earth. Each phrase conveys a purpose and a testimony. These verses are born from the poetics of crisis, as a response to devastation.

In recent years, Begoña Ugalde has moved from the crisis of intimacy—body, home, femininity, motherhood, romantic love—to an exploration of the ecological crisis, assuming that perhaps both arise from the same root. This work belongs to this last stage, in which the poems acquire a broader scope that probes the fractures and scars of the environment.

My heart is an active volcano

To learn or try to translate
the quiet language of the Andes
its paths populated
by endemic shrubs
whose names I can't pronounce
I go on all fours like a mountain animal
seeking to escape from predators
to find new refuges
caves of stone and shade

When I take shelter in the vegetation
my skin abandons its narrative of scars
and sun marks from birth
become a little like a spring
a little cracked
I talk about small flowers
species resistant to neglect
that only need sunlight
water that drains through the aquifers
and then becomes a torrent or a rainbow again

I continue slowly upward
because it's hard to carry so many layers
of clothing it's hard to carry a bunch of keys
a house that no longer exists

I have no choice but to heed
the call of my muscles
their cramps their tiredness
from decades of dedication
to others who are not me
but are also me

Then I abandon all backpacks
I refresh my tongue with succulents
and geophytes of impossible beauty

I look closely at the soft tissue
that contains and limits me
in the weave of my arms
I discover shooting stars
rare constellations
southern crosses
underground streams
roads forking
to lives that were not mine

I can't find another way to say it:
my heart is an active volcano
about to erupt

I hide inside my chest
a rugged geography

I fear tachycardia
the next earthquake
becoming a river of dark lava
forest covered in ash

Rapid breathing song moan
coming from my cracked lips
when I draw strength from the landscape
to continue attempting the ascent

I perceive the short phrases as if from other
that I manage to utter when I catch my breath
calming the runaway pulse wild horse
crossing the border
without load or saddle

I sweat out my sorrow
I go from solid to liquid
from doubt to certainty to delirium
I become corn
gravel suspended dust erosion

and in that vapor I perceive cloud
Is it perhaps a warmth
I recover from the thunder?
my own moisture suspended
in the air and its apparent emptiness?

I rest my gaze on the brilliance
that sustains the river
and its transparent songs
on the shore I have a long talk with me
I understand myself part of the invisible
mineral   plant   and animal kingdoms

I accept once and for all
that nothing ever stops changing
that nothing ever stops changing
that nothing ever stops changing

dazzled by the brilliance
of the glacier maybe eternal
I fluctuate between the desire
for physical contact
and the obsidian edge

I close the momentary blindness
that fatigue gives me
I surrender without fear to the waters
newborn from the thaw

I finally quench my thirst
with a crystalline thread
that dances between the cracks
and traces a small diverted river
a prayer that is erased
at the same time as it is written

on the snow-covered slope
I draw with my fingertips
fables that thaw
from another celestial imagination
like objects that reappear
when summer begins

I take stock of what
the path offers me:
broken bottles
pieces of glass
blue green water amber yellow
orphan shoes with wooden soles
blunt knives that refract
the silent routes of the sun

I avoid collecting tools
that other explorers have abandoned
I only treasure hallucination as a way of life
arid concepts that later become ferment
evening primroses bulbs wild lilies
that are born and burn at the same time

and a fluorescent alpaca blanket
that covers my face
from the dust that rises
when I drag it up the hill
turning it the flag
of no country

At the summit an unprecedented panorama
is revealed: ethereal beings that populate the slopes
make me witness to their timeless dialogues
breezes and gusts that envelop everything

The mountain range seems sculpted
like a many-winged night butterfly
storm-colored ruin
vestige of when the whole earth
was one open temple

I concentrate listening to the echo
of the echo of the echo of the echo
I pursue its last resonances
I offer it all my confusion

fall away like boulders
the presages of collapse
another current of air enters my pores
oxygenates the future
dissolves the partial cloudiness of my old ideas
about that which possesses language
a telluric sound
emerges from the cracked ground
reveals detours and shortcuts
that I mark on my internal map

from above loses meaning
the score of the thoughts
so contrary to the whisper
of what breathes deeply and resists

like the lichen that clings to the stone
when drought is the law
I shiver with my whole body
I see myself blurred on the earth
and everything that grows on it

undertaking any journey
involves watching your pasture burn
renouncing a kind of protection
to your mother tongue
its vocabulary conceived so far away

my writing is intuitive archaeology
the corpse of a llama
that encloses a treasure an amulet
the accumulation of a gasp
a stone that I take out of my stomach
and throw forcefully toward the ravine

I rehearse new spells
I appreciate perspectives
that come from a soft noise
remainders of the Andean carnival
that neither deafens nor it scares

Lightly I embrace a glow before everything
because this is an inverse text
without beginning or end
that serves to cure
all the ills we carry within

At times I hold other stones
tinted calypso by the weeping of copper
I enclose my breath in my hands
my fingerprints finally recover
the sense of touch

I wish to bear witness to the frost
of its ancient intimacy with the rocks
of my own intimacy withdrawn
toward a cold that burns inside

I try to translate the correspondence
of the peaks with the south wind
I compose verses that are matter
that changes state
as we occasionally change names
houses skin and appearance

I try to imitate the condor
that spreads and unfurls
its storm-gray feathers
to cross like a letter without a sender
the sky the certain possibility
of a suspended home

but I choose to be carrion
that surrenders to death
without resistance

I enjoy the fall
the edges of what seems rough
hard or immutable
become soft and blur
like the light on the ravine
just before the day dies

I summon from the howl
other hands and mouths
queñuas and llaretas
oxygen and hydrogen
vertigo and euphoria
new ways
of loving the abyss

GABRIELA RUIVO

Translated from Portugal Portuguese by Gilles Madan

'Then, very slowly, my branches disappeared and I knew that it was time to bury myself in the sand, not to die, but to dissolve into the granular multitude, and run, like water, to the ocean where I would be born.'

Gabriela is an award-winning Portuguese poet and novelist whose work explores the lingering effects of psychological trauma, womanhood, and the boundaries of nature and self. These prose-poems are from her 2022 collection, 'A Woman of her Word' (Uma Mulher de Palavra). Ruivo is active in the UK as a co-founder of the Portuguese in Translation Book Club, a group meeting bi-monthly on Zoom to discuss books by Portuguese-language authors translated into English, and the Clube das Mulheres Escritoras (Women Writers' Club), an initiative aiming to promote the work of contemporary Portuguese female authors. I worked directly with the author on this project, incorporating her feedback into the translations.

I've selected these poems because they respond to the notion of 'correspondences between outer territory and inner self', fusing natural elements with emotions and landscapes of the body. In an economically driven society that values profit over sustainability, taking advantage of vulnerable populations while plundering the land and resources, Gabriela's poems speak directly to the acceleration of violence in the news cycle and the effects of climate change. They search for a language to express individual and collective suffering, a language that can help us reconnect with ourselves and the natural worlds we inhabit.

Bird nature

One day, a long time ago, I dreamt I was a bird. But, confused, I noticed the years passed and my promised wings didn't grow. I tried to hold onto earthly certainties. With enormous effort, I forced branches with dizzying shadows to grow where my arms had been and deep roots out of the soles of my feet. I stood there, ecstatic, while all around me the biggest desert I had ever known burst open: a desert that emerged from me with the force of a gale. I emptied out completely, until I was unrecognisable. Then, very slowly, my branches disappeared and I knew that it was time to bury myself in the sand, not to die, but to dissolve into the granular multitude, and run, like water, to the ocean where I would be born. It was there, amidst the waves, that I found your eyes. For a long time, I thought it was those eyes that saved me, but I was wrong. Your fisheyes only opened mine and dyed them blue, a colour that was absent in the desert I came from. And no, your arms didn't save me; mine did. It was those dried out branches that floated in the water making invisible primordial gestures, useless now, while I evaporated and freed myself from the dark earth. Now, in the echoes of shells and tides, I hear distant voices in the ocean. My bird nature is calling for me, waving to me with its wide wings: the wings I dreamt of having instead of arms since the beginning of time.

Die standing

They say stars, like candles, burn until the very end. They say trees, like stars, burn while standing, until the very end. And before they do, they expand into infinity, staining the red of wounds with blood, the green of withered leaves with sap.

RIFAT ABBAS, ASHU LAL, & SANWAL GURMANI, AND TAUQIR REZA

Translated from Sairaki and Panjabi by Mediah Ahmed

This selection, 'Nature's Rhythmical Rebellion: Musical resistance of fields, rivers and skies', is in two parts: Saraiki poetry, with poems by Rifat Abbas, Ashu Lal and Sanwal Gurmani, and Panjabi poetry, with three poems by Tauqir Reza. The selected poems explore themes of ancestral memory, ecological intimacy, poetic resistance, and political truth-telling—carried by the rhythms of land, longing, and rebellion.

My selection is rooted in the languages, imagery, and pulse of the land—moving between Panjabi and Saraiki, across rivers, fields, wounds, and skies. These translations are not only linguistic but emotional attempts to carry the rhythm and soul of each poem into English, while attending to the landscape that shaped them. Nature's own rhythms create music together with the defiant voices of the land's people.

The six poems included are:
1. 'Kafi' (Sanwal Gurmani), which explores love, longing, and the politics of peace through music and wilderness metaphors,
2. 'We Drum in Your Name' (after Ashu Lal), a translation-adaption poem capturing Ashu Lal's poetic rebellion, inspired by his tone and vision,
3. 'Kafi' (after Rifat Abbas), a reflection on bodily memory and ancestral longing tied deeply to rural Saraiki landscapes,
4. 'Miracles of Technology' (Tauqir Reza), a sharp, surreal critique of modernity, land, and delusion,
5. 'The Silence of the Sky' (Tauqir Reza), a lament for truth-tellers, martyred and unheard, and
6. 'O Sky! Be Afraid of That Moment' (Tauqir Reza), a warning to power about the eventual eruption of buried rage.

I am currently deepening my practice as a translator by studying classical Panjabi poets. I'm transliterating Waris Shah's *Heer* and am part of a group translating Mian Muhammad Bakhsh's *Saif al-Mulūk*. This has led me to discover and connect with contemporary poets like those above. Through this process, I hope to translate not just words, but textures—rhythms, silences, and the sensory depth of poems that feel like home.

Nature's Rhythmical Rebellion:
Musical resistance of fields, rivers and skies

Kafi
(after Rifat Abbas)

Where, oh where, flows the river Indus?
Where, oh where, is my beloved?

Where, oh where, did the people cross bridges and vanish?
Where, oh where, did the boats drift with time,
and the wind ferry them from this shore to the next?

Where, oh where, do the lights glow in God's village?
Where does the sun rise over the luminous barren sands of the Divine?
Where, oh where, does the beloved awaken?

Where, oh where, are the dolphins of Indus joyful,
the fish leaping with gladness?
The story of the blue-throated flower sings,
even the Black Drongo caws in delight—
a chorus of cranes takes flight—where, oh where?

Within mosques, within temples, calls echo together.
They left with Ram, together with all the saints of God.
Alive, still alive, is your eternal lifeforce—
O wearer of life's garland—where, oh where are you?

Rifat Abbas's kafi delves deep into the sacred and the earthly, pulling on the threads of both spiritual reverence and the natural world. His words offer a direct communion with the landscape, evoking the sacred geography of Sindh—the river Indus, the thriving wildlife, the divine light of villages. These elements converge, not as separate entities, but as one living, breathing existence. The kafi reminds us of the profound connection between humanity, the divine, and the environment, illustrating a world where life flows harmoniously through both the physical and spiritual realms.

This translation draws on the call-and-response pattern found in the original, the repeated 'Where, oh where?' highlighting the search for meaning, for connection, for the divine in every corner of existence. Through this poem, Rifat Abbas's plea is not only for a return to the natural and sacred origins of life but also a cry for unity and remembrance, drawing a bridge between the ecological and the ethereal.

We Drum in Your Name
(after Ashu Lal)

Green-green acacia trees,
are adorned with white-white bugs that hum.
We think people are simple—
you just see only thugs all around, my beloved.

Rain falls gently
on fields, on flowers, and on buds—
slowly, slowly, within the soul,
a fire drums with its sorrows.

Eyes are swollen, my love—
why have you turned away, my love?
We are quiet like the faqirs—
but the whole world rages at your silence.

Where is the moon of nine nights?
Where are those seven or eight years?
Aeons and aeons have passed by—
I began drumming in your name.

We are your sons, we are your daughters, O Sindhu,
your breath, your aorta, your life: we your children.
We carry our honour in your name—
we tie turbans in your beloved name.

This poem is a translation-adaptation of a Saraiki kafi by the revolutionary poet Ashu Lal. His poetry often embodies deep-rooted land memory, spiritual resistance, and ancestral connection. In 'We Drum in Your Name', the imagery of rain, drums, and turbans becomes a metaphor for generational longing, collective grief, and the heartbeat of the land. Translating this was both a challenge and a privilege—I've tried to remain true to the cultural soul while opening a window into its emotional cadence. It's a song of Sindhu, of honour, loss, and identity—of the rhythm that binds us back to earth.

Kafi
(after Sanwal Gurmani)

I sent word to my beloved—
a message to return.

The forest frets endlessly
to own its newborn deer.

A wall was built before anger,
begin to create a song anew.

We are merely passing through—
let us walk the path of love.

With the beloved,
on a bed dyed red—
this is the cost of being born to earth.

The task of love's naghaaraa, O Sanwal,
is to silence every war,
to still all conflict.

This Kafi by Sanwal Gurmani pulses with the rhythms of love, land, and longing. Set against the backdrop of nature—the forest, the deer, the red earth—it weaves the emotional terrain of human connection into the physical landscape. The forest's anxiety for its fawn mirrors our own vulnerabilities, while the path of love becomes a metaphorical journey across the land. The naghaaraa of love, traditionally used in communal celebrations and declarations, is reimagined here as an instrument of peace—resolving wars through rhythm and resonance. In a world increasingly marked by conflict, this poem calls us back to tenderness, rootedness, and reconciliation—the true rhythms of the land and heart alike.

Miracles of Technology

(Tauqir Reza)

After spitting on the dusty face of earth,
They are going to kiss, the soils of the moon and Mars.
Digging foundations.
Constructing the rooftops of future generations.
It's a good thing,
But what has the earth done wrong?
Whose body,
Trembling with the roar of rockets and warplanes constantly,
Whose chest is uprooted by the chains of war tanks,
Ears deafen by bomb blasts,
The smoke of motorcars blinding eyes.
Whose mountains! Devoured by the blackened witch of roads,
Whose trees! Swallowed by Samri's factory,
(In the name of mineral water),
Whose waters
Are emptied in one gulp by the magic bag of clever 'Amro 'Ayyaar,
(And over there,
the East and West fall asleep,
Whilst waiting for the return of Jesus and Mahdi,
After witnessing the miracles of technology
Read the declaration of faith in science)

'Miracles of Technology' explores the tensions between human progress and the earth's delicate balance. The poem reflects on how technological advancements, such as rockets, warplanes, and motorcars, have altered not just the physical landscape but also the spiritual and environmental fabric of the world. It meditates on the destruction of nature, the impact of industrialisation, and the neglect of the earth's cries, while also questioning the future of humanity as it embraces these 'miracles' of technology. The poem speaks to the rhythm of human actions and their consequences on the land, emphasising the clash between modernity and the environment.

Silence of the Sky
(Tauqir Reza)

O truthful ones!
For speaking the truth,
this was the punishment we received—
while lies were smeared across our foreheads.
The moment we began to write the truth,
nails were hammered into our hands.
The crosses were dyed in our blood,
yet we did not lose heart.
We were told that God always stands with the truth—
(and we kept walking, believing it).

O truthful ones!
We were broken, from then—
when vultures started eating our brains,
and eagles carried away the light of our eyes.
Our truth was looted, stripped again and again,
but no unseen hand lifted us
from the cross into the sky, no heart was resurrected.
(Perhaps our truth was too heavy to bear.)

And when our bodies—
were being buried into the earth,
at that very moment,
Jesus was neither on the mountain
nor on the cross.
And the sky—
like Mary—
remained silent.

This poem by Tauqir Reza is a searing meditation on the cost of truth-telling in a world where lies are rewarded and resistance is punished. As I translated it from Panjabi, I was struck by its spiritual register—how the crucifixion, vultures, and silent sky all become metaphors for systemic violence and divine absence. The truth here is not abstract; it is embodied, bleeding, buried. Translating it meant carrying the emotional weight of its silences and defiant laments, while trying to echo its rhythm and tenderness in English. In Reza's imagery, I felt echoes of Karbala, Golgotha and countless unnamed graves.

O Sky! Be Afraid of That Moment
(after Tauqir Reza)

O sky!
Let your rains fall—
let them wash the spilled blood from the earth.
But do not be so sure
the fire within us
has been extinguished by these raindrops.

Fear that moment—
when once again,
from the green thread of life,
a red flame bursts into being.
Water in smoke-filled eyes,
starts to blaze—
forged in the heat of boiling blood—
will gather
into dark red clouds
that thunder across your head.

This poem by Tauqir Reza is a warning to oppressive forces cloaked
in elemental imagery. The sky is addressed directly, not only as a
witness to violence but as a potential accomplice through its silence
and deluge. Translating this piece meant holding the tension
between elemental and emotional registers—the 'green thread of life'
(ساوی ناڑ) as both delicate and resilient, the fire that smoulders in
the ears as a symbol of buried rage. I kept the invocation 'O sky!' and
the original's formal intensity to preserve the poem's urgent tone,
where nature becomes both metaphor and participant in the
struggle for justice.

ALI ASADOLLAHI

Translated from Farsi by the author

This poem reflects on environmental devastation in Iran and its wider global implications. The poem appears in my fourth collection of Persian poetry, *Bonbaste-Fereshteh* (بن‌بست فرشته : 'Dead End of the Angel'), published in Iran in 2017. This poem is dedicated to the jailed environmental activists in Iran, including individuals such as Kavous Seyed-Emami, who tragically died in custody under suspicious circumstances. Their detention, often on unfounded charges of espionage, underscores the significant personal and political risks associated with documenting environmental destruction in Iran, where censorship is pervasive. In this context, poetry offers a vital space to evoke and sustain a sense of belonging and memory in the face of suppression that can lead to numbness and indifference.

I Used to Dream, I Used to be Safe

For Lake Urmia, which dried up within ten years
for Hyrcanian forests turning into ashes
and for five environmental experts detained from January 2018
to March 2024 in Iran

Give me a sign.
I remember such a blue sky
that gave me a sign.
When the world is immersed in smoke,
give me a sign.
Remember me
somewhere beyond the mountains,
beyond the seas and burnt bodies.
I was a stranger
in the purity of the red-breasted robin's crop
or in a small rabbit's mouth.
Face to face, you were so alluring
that green dripped from your leaves.
And at the time of farewell,
if my body, as free as grains of sand, slips
through your slender fingers,
give me a sign.
Open your mouth and say love
is something else.
Show me the stem, the moss,
dance me on the snake scales, and slip.
You flare and ask: what happened to us?
I kiss you:
let's sleep and forget.

You remember that morning?
All houses beyond the windows are burnt.
The fields of ashes, before us
there is no sound.
The scenery's black and red.
The world's silence resembles
a Christmas morning after heavy snow
and the wind passes through gashes on our faces.
My alluring one,
more alluring than the otherworldliness
of a female fox
in killing cold, placing her teats
to her blind pups' mouths.
That fox is killed.
And the mother's eyes' movement
for the last look at the babies
itself needed a requiem.
We didn't have enough poems,
a poem for the pupils of that fox,
a poem comparing your smile
to a boiling Qanat, you see?
A virgin Qanat under a virgin palm tree
if someone cries on its poisoned cap.
Oh the water of life it was.
The fountain of youth it was.
Give me a sign.
A poem for the annihilated wings of a crane:
two wings
with the pride of two meters,
wide open in a grey eternity.
The last crane, free and free,

ALI ASADOLLAHI **99**

left wing! The left wing has been shot!
A poem for a crash
with thousands of terrified passengers.
What happened to us?
Take shelter in my arms,
free me with a deep sleep.
Let's sleep and when we
wake up we won't chew our flesh ever again.
Your mouth was full too, you
remember?
My alluring one,
does the pearl of your sparkling teeth
soothe the pain of a sheep
whose lamb you have torn on the plate?
With each of your kisses on a cigarette,
somewhere the tobacco fields are burning.
Will you chew me too?
Stand up like a cypress that burns
green and its honest flames
can be seen in the wilderness.
Remember me
that I'm all your passed-away ones,
blown in a foggy breeze.
In the morning that without
tears, without smile, without anger,
hope and despair
you opened your eyes and
said what happened to us?
Ashes on mirrors.
The burners are suspended in the air.

Look at me,
look how I sway in the wind, free and free.
Disaster was falling
and the living were escaping
from one hole to another.
Disaster was pouring
and we were burning and chewing.
Pour me a glass of oil,
a glass of blood.
Pour out what you have to pour to
remember:
a sip of molten salt
in the throat of a lake,
a sharpened pencil
in the plantain's muscle,
a bit of lead for the tiger,
a little fish flopping on the ground,
toads,
dragonflies,
eagles,
plains,
a piece of desert and a
piece of river.
On the other side,
a roaring sea for ever and ever.
A poem for every newborn microbe,
another one and another
newcomers: chewers.
A poem for the agonizing
of a giant round and blue body
saturated with crazy growth of microbes.

A poem for the end of food sources
in the patient's body,
an elegy for hungry germs,
falling viruses,
a prose for recovery,
an ode for later.
Let's sleep and forget.

N.S. SIGOGO

Translated from isiNdebele by Stephen Walsh

I have been fitfully translating Sigogo's poetry for some time as a kind
of cultural thank you for some happy and formative years living in
Bulawayo in the 1980s. It was a time of great excitement; I was a new
teacher and Zimbabwe was a new country. 1983 was The Year of
Transformation, according to the government, but the old men used
to fret about the dissolution of Ndebele culture in the face of a
variety of challenges. Giving these poems a little transformation of
my own feels like giving something back.

Sigogo's prose works are set text standards read widely in schools,
but his poems, scattered in various pre- and post-independence
anthologies, are harder to find. Like this one, they often reflect a life
rooted in the landscape and traditional values of the rural world into
which he was born. The language of the original is quite rhetorical
and performative, though the stanzas are regular with occasional
rhyme. By 'elasticising' the English syntax, while introducing the
ghost of a rhyme, I hope I've achieved some kind of approximation to
the feeling of cornucopia of the poem.

I vividly remember Sigogo, by then a smiling public man, visiting
the school where I worked. Afterwards we shared a bucket of beer in
the garden of the shebeen across the road. The joy at the end of this
poem is mine as well as his.

Ehlobo ('Summer')

Summer-growth's green, boundless, stretching free.
Stretching my heart's bounds. Rivers, full, fill it up too.
    And sorghum, new-ready in my uncle's fields,
    Takes me to fields my great-grandfathers had.

The women singing, sweet, as they pick the green corn.
Children's mouths. Cows, by rivers, eat with mouths too.
    The careless grass lying on the roads is
    An offering to the drizzling rain. To joy.

Forestfuls of flowers. Of bees. Of animal rejoicing
At the green corn. Creatures of mountain, of rocks too,
    Come out to ape the beasts of the wood
    By taking cool water at the river's edge.

All creatures finding their food. One eats another: each
To each, the biter bit. The mountains squaring up too.
    They stand tall, each to each—two sons
    Who will fight for their forefathers' lands.

My nose, flaring, breathing freshest air. My veins,
Themselves like flowing rivers, set my blood free too.
    Love's soul-rivers flow, burst their banks,
    Overflow with the milk of kindness.

Creatures coming where the red fruits will be ripe.
To the river. People and all living things too.
    Walking on foot and beating the air,
    For the forest is the field of the nations.

Birds singing from the treetops that cover the rivers.
Evergreen branches that bend to drink too—
    To drink the water from the pools,
    To drink in the songs of the birds.

Sometimes, myself, I see myself singing. Singing
A song that summer taught me but is unknown too.
    I do not sing well. My voice is hoarse.
    But I drink beer. And sing with joy.

ALI AKKOUR

Translated from Arabic by Alaa Alqaisi

What first drew me to this poem was its quiet devastation—how it renders grief inseparable from geography. The poem speaks in a low, mournful voice, where landscape, body, and myth collapse into each other.

In translating عرق سيزيف I opted for 'The sinews of Sisyphus' to keep both the physical labour and the mythic burden alive, threading Greek myth into the soil of Arabic poetry. I also kept the rhythm close to the original, using line breaks and spacing to echo the pauses and quiet swell of the Arabic.

Most crucially, I preserved the final image—'the finger that once wounded and vanished'—as a haunting trace of forgotten violence. The entire poem, for me, moves like water carrying memory: some things float, others sink, but none stay still.

The Lakes Remember Nothing,
Nor the Rivers

I walk—fused with her—
listening
to the hush she folds around her depths,
without a mourning breath
This land:
a vast and aching body,
lets loose a gasp in the heights,
a sigh across the stripped-down plains.
The sinews of Sisyphus
still rise,
surging in every ancient well.
Her sorrow is older than memory.
The lakes remember nothing of what made them weep,
and the rivers—
no longer capable
of naming the finger
that once wounded them—
then disappeared.

SUBHRO BANDOPADHYAY

Translated from Bengali by Sampurna Chattarji

This poem from contemporary Bengali poet Subhro Bandopadhyay's *Osharlipi* (Srishtisukh, January 2023, Kolkata, India) raises, among others, a tricky and potentially disruptive question—how can one continue to write in a beloved mother tongue while acknowledging that it is numb and aching with the stupor of ages? As he locates and unpacks the history, geography, physiognomy and psychology of Bengali a.k.a. Bangla, he establishes a series of investigations into the nature of the connection between the land from which the language springs, and the landing it makes in the listening heart.

The 'rhythms of the land' that is Bengal are tuned as much to the hum of the past as they are to the ricochets of the present. Bangla is a place, as slumberous as heat-numbed villages, as shackled to seasons and habits as its people. As Bandopadhyay attempts to unsettle and undo that burdensome lethargy, he writes, 'This is our Bangla, woken up again / By the unaccustomed sound of other languages'.

Through the systolic/diastolic beat of his language, inextricably embedded in landscape, Bandopadhyay also reflects upon the often-unacknowledged hybridity of Bangla (reflected in the form of his collection, dense prose paragraphs alternating with looser sections visually delineated in the manner we expect from traditional poetry) and the unspeakable damage done to the rivers and the villages that are seen as no more than meat for conquest and consumption. Neither eulogy not lament, his texts are both provocation and speculation, confronting monstrous foam-jungles, sandy roads scattered with metallic arrays, long river-roads on which abandoned boats float. Scenes of ecological devastation suggest a greater, deeper, more invisible rupture between individual and community, nature and technology, the settled and the uprooted.

As a contemporary Indian poet who writes in English and

translates from Bangla, I feel uniquely stirred by a dangerous challenge I can only embrace with delight—to convey Bandopadhyay's intentions in and through one of those 'other languages' whose colonial histories cast such a long (but no longer dreaded!) shadow over all of us who write from and about India.

Atmosphere

Repeatedly October descends
On villages   deep rivers   jungles
Waiting and silence
Asphyxia and union
Repeatedly the sky's autumn turns its head
Towards the meat of greed

Village roots   bodies   songs
Roads   festivals   waterlessness
Have unfurled before them existence
And into their mouths descends
The shadowfree meat of October

This is our Bangla, woken up again
By the unaccustomed sound of other languages
Though even now the meat of a few old phrases still clings

The uprooting of a multitude of villages can clearly be heard
Day of incredible sun, phrases worn out by disuse
Goodbye messages in an unaccustomed language
Pages of grammar spiked on nails
Rising in grotesque metallic sound

The uprooting of years and days can be heard
Catatonia comes and touches wholeness
Meat-eating birds can be seen
Tearing hunks from the flesh of massive villages
The bodies of massive rivers

Village and town   practise and partition   could clearly be heard
Prepared reading lists and repudiation
Boycotted words and my own-ness
Uprooting of that fixed gazing towards the stars

Thousands of meat-eating birds were heard
Who in truth are carrying away crematoria and carrion-dumps
       from chockful skies
Carrying away the mounds of our neglect

Have they taken me too? The entire sky is the belly
Of a snake swollen with villages swallowed whole
Leaving behind
The sloughed-off skin of my language   unlettered

NOTES ON CONTRIBUTORS

AKAGI KOBAYASHI has had a long career as a professional interpreter/ translator in the UK, Ireland and Japan, with most of her output in the technical and business world. She has translated poems, haiku and tanka into and out of Japanese, and also writes them bilingually. She is a member of UK's Institute of Translation and Interpreting, and Association of Translators & Interpreters Ireland.

ALAA ALQAISI is a Palestinian translator and writer. Fluent in Arabic and English, she holds an MA in Translation Studies and has over a decade of experience in literary and cultural translation. She has translated poetry by contemporary authors, and her translations have appeared or are forthcoming in *ArabLit*, and other literary platforms. She has also translated two poems into Arabic for the poet Akaiser.

ALI AKKOUR is a Saudi poet and writer known for his lyrical voice and evocative imagery. He has published a collection of very short stories titled *The Biography of Things*, and three poetry collections: *Mail for the Trees of September*, *Like a Small Victory for Lightning and Tremble*, and *Your Absence Is a Member of the Family*. His most recent work is a poetic play titled *Dialogue Between the Rose and the Wind*.

ALI ASADOLLAHI is an award-winning Iranian poet and author of six Persian poetry collections, based in Tehran. He holds a Master's degree in Persian Literature, and is a permanent member of the Iranian Writers' Association (established in 1968). He has received multiple national poetry awards in Iran and has led various poetry workshops at universities and institutions across the country.

ALTON MELVAR M. DAPANAS, from the southern Philippines, is the author of *M of the Southern Downpours* (Australia: Downingfield Press, 2024), *In the Name of the Body: Lyric Essays* (Canada: Wrong

Publishing, 2023), and *Towards a Theory on City Boys: Prose Poems* (UK: Newcomer Press, 2021). Their works appear in the anthologies *Infinite Constellations* (University of Alabama Press) and *He, She, They, Us: Queer Poems* (Pan Macmillan UK).

ANNA YIN was Mississauga's inaugural Poet Laureate (2015–2017) and has authored six poetry collections and four books of translations. Her work has appeared in *Queen's Quarterly, ARC Poetry*, the *New York Times, China Daily*, CBC Radio and the *World Journal*. She has read at Parliament Hill, the Austin International Poetry Festival and the Edmonton Poetry Festival. Her next book will be published by Frontenac Press.

ASHU LAL, a qualified medical doctor, is also a radical poet, thinker, and cultural icon whose Saraiki verse challenges orthodoxy and questions power. His work blends mysticism, rebellion, and human dignity in a voice that has inspired generations of progressive readers. His short story collection, *Abnormal*, has recently been translated into Urdu by Aks Publications.

BEGOÑA UGALDE studied Hispanic Literature at the University of Chile and Literary Creation at the Universitat Pompeu Fabra. Her poetry collections include *La fiesta vacía, Poemas sobre mi normalidad, Lunares, La virgen de las Antenas*, and *El cielo de los animales*, and she is also author of the short story collections *Es lo que hay* and *Economía de guerra*, as well as numerous theatrical works.

BILL COYLE's publications include the poetry collection *The God of This World to His Prophet*, which won the New Criterion Poetry Prize, and a volume of translations of the Swedish poet Håkan Sandell, *Dog Star Notations: Selected Poems 1999–2016*.

CINDY A. VELASQUEZ is a professor at the University of San Carlos in Cebu City, Philippines. She has edited the anthology *Dagat ug Kinabuhi* ('Sea and Life'): *Translating Contemporary Cebuano Poetry* and written an illustrated children's book series on ethno-medicinal practices of the indigenous Ati community. She is also a songwriter; with Jude Gitamondoc, she won the 43rd Gawad Urian Award for Best Music in 2020.

CLAUDIA MAGLIANO was born in Montevideo, Uruguay in 1974. She is a professor of literature at the Instituto de Profesores Artigas. In 2005 she received placed first in a contest for unpublished poetry organized by the Casa de los Escritores del Uruguay, which led to the publication of *Nada* ('Nothing'). In 2010, Ático Ediciones published her book *Res* ('Cow'), which received a prize from the Uruguayan Ministry of Education and Culture.

DALIA TAHA is a Palestinian poet, playwright, and educator with an MFA in Playwriting from Brown University. Taha has published three poetry books, a novel, two plays, and a children's poetry book. Her plays have been staged at the Royal Court Theatre in London and the Flemish Royal Theatre in Brussels, and elsewhere. Her poetry collection, *Enter World*, will be published in 2025 by Almutawassit Publishing House, and in English translation by Graywolf Press in 2026. She lives in Ramallah.

DRAGO YURAC (Santiago de Chile, 1996–) has published the poetry book *El esplendor oculto* (Pez Espiral, 2024), and translations of Lydia Tomkiw, Penny Rimbaud, Yone Noguchi, and D. H. Lawrence. She organized the reading series 'Buenas noches, poetas' (Good night, poets) in tribute to the poet Pedro Montealegre (2023 and 2024). She is currently pursuing a Master's in Creative Writing at Universitat

Pompeu Fabra (Barcelona), while working on her next book of sentimental chronicles.

ELENA SALAMANCA combines literature, performance and memory in public spaces and advocates for rights of women and girls in Central America. Her poetry collections include *[INCOGNITA FLORA CUSCATLANICA]* (2025), *Tal vez monstruos* ('Monsters Maybe', 2022) and *Landsmoder* (2022). She is a three-time recipient of the National Poetry Prize in El Salvador. Currently, she is a doctoral candidate in History at El Colegio de México.

ELLEN CORBETT is a translator and current PhD Researcher at Ulster University. She holds a Bachelor of Arts International in German and Léann an Aistriúcháin (Irish Translation Studies) from the University of Galway (formerly NUI Galway), and a Master's in Translation Studies from Queen's University, Belfast. She is the 2024 winner of the Stephen Spender Prize for poetry in translation.

EMI MIYAOKA is a Japanese poet and Hirakata city official. In Japan, she has published the books *THE BIRD'S WISH, IT FLIES SILENTLY* (Minatonohito, 2012) and *BEYOND THE BORDER* (Shichosha, 2015). The musical album *Parallel Motion, Flying Cats' Silence* sets four poems from these books to music for a mixed chorus and piano.

ERIKA MIHÁLYCSA teaches modern and contemporary Irish and British literature at Babeş-Bolyai University, Cluj, Romania. She has published mostly on Joyce, Beckett, translation studies and various aspects of European literary and visual modernism. She has translated fiction by Flann O'Brien, Beckett, Patrick McCabe and others into Hungarian and a handful of modern and contemporary Hungarian authors into English.

GABRIELA RUIVO is a Portuguese author based in Scotland. Her works include the novels *Uma Outra Voz* and *Lei da Gravidade*, the poetry collections *Aves Migratórias* and *Uma Mulher de Palavra*, and the short story collection *Espécies Protegidas*. She manages Miúda Books, an online bookshop specialising in children's literature written in Portuguese, and is the head of AILD Cultural Team (International Association of Luso Descendants) in the UK.

GILLES MADAN is an emerging Portuguese-English translator and member of PELTA (Portuguese-English Literary Translator's Association). He has an MA in Poetry and Poetics from the University of York.

GIZELLA HERVAY (1934–1982) was a Hungarian-Romanian poet and translator. Sometimes termed 'the Ingeborg Bachmann of Transylvania', she grew up in a very poor family and experienced a difficult childhood. Mostly neglected by criticism during her life, she started publishing in the most important Hungarian-language magazines in Romania in the 1960s. Hervay was awarded the Prize for Hungarian Art posthumously in 1993.

HÅKAN SANDELL was born in 1962 in Malmö, in southern Sweden, and has lived since the mid-90s in Oslo, Norway. He is the author of 25 collections of poetry, the most recent of which is *Under jagande moln* ('Under Racing Clouds', 2025).

HILARY BIRD (1948–) lives and works in Estonia. She is the author of *An introduction to Estonian literature* (Slavica, Indiana University, 2018), an historical anthology of Estonian literature that includes translations of work by 60 writers from ancient times to 1991, and has translated established poets from Estonian to English, including Doris Kareva and Paul-Erik Rummo, as well as younger poets such as Maarja Pärtna.

JEANNINE MARIE PITAS is the translator or co-translator of twelve Latin American books, most recently Uruguayan poet Silvia Guerra's *A Sea at Dawn*, co-translated with Jesse Lee Kercheval and published in 2023 by Eulalia Books, where she now serves as editor.

JESSE LEE KERCHEVAL is a poet and translator, specializing in Uruguayan poetry. Her translations include *Love Poems* by Idea Vilariño and *The Invisible Bridge: Selected Poems of Circe Maia*, for which she was awarded an NEA in Translation, both published by the University of Pittsburgh Press. She is the editor of the Wisconsin Poetry Series at the University of Wisconsin Press.

KENZABURŌ ŌE was the author of *Warera no kyōki wo ikinobiru michi wo oshieyo* ('Teach Us to Outgrow Our Madness'), *Memushiri kōchi* ('Nip the Buds, Shoot the Kids'), *Kojinteki na taiken* ('A Personal Matter') and other works considered classics in Japan. In 1994 he was awarded the Nobel Prize in Literature for his 'poetic force [that] creates an imagined world, where life and myth condense to form a disconcerting picture of the human predicament today'.

LAOIGHSEACH NÍ CHOISTEALBHA was born in 1994 and raised in the Laggan in East Donegal. She now lives in the Conamara Gaeltacht. *Solas Geimhridh agus Dánta Eile* (Barzaz, 2023) is her first collection, and her second collection, *Mainistir na Feola*, is forthcoming with Barzaz (2025).

MAARJA PÄRTNA (b.1986) is an Estonian poet and translator. She has won major literary awards in Estonia, was City Writer of Tartu in 2024, the year the city was a UNESCO City of Literature, and has organized literary events both in Estonia and abroad.

MAGDA SZÉKELY (1936–2007), born in Budapest to an assimilated Jewish family, was eight years old when she witnessed her mother being dragged away by fascists; she herself survived the Holocaust hidden first in a Catholic monastery and then by a Swabian family. Her first volume of poetry *Kőtabla* ('Stone Tablet') was published in 1962, and altogether she was the author of nine volumes of poetry and the recipient of numerous prizes.

MARINA TSVETAEVA was born in Moscow in 1892. Her first collection of poems, *Evening Album*, attracted the attention of leading poets and critics. After suffering great hardship in post-revolutionary Moscow, she joined her husband in exile in 1922. In 1939 she returned to the Soviet Union and was evacuated to the provincial town of Elabuga in the wake of the Nazi invasion. She committed suicide in 1941.

MEDIAH AHMED is a poet, researcher, and translator with an academic background in astrophysics and biophysics. She is currently working on translating regional poetic traditions from Panjab into English, focusing on Saraiki and Panjabi poetries.

N.S. SIGOGO (Ndabezinhle Sibanda Sigogo) (1932–2006) is the best-known writer of isiNdebele, the minority language of south-west Zimbabwe.

OTTILIE MULZET has translated the work of László Krasznahorkai, Szilárd Borbély, Gábor Schein, Krisztina Tóth, Edina Szvoren, László Földényi, István Vörös, György Dragomán and others. In 2019 she was awarded the National Book Award for Translated Literature for her translation of László Krasznahorkai's novel *Baron Wenckheim's Homecoming*.

PIEDAD BONNETT is a Colombian poet, winner of the Premio Reina Sofía for Latin American poetry and Colombia's National Poetry Prize. She is the author of nine collections of poetry, as well as novels, plays and short stories. Among her best-known works is the memoir, *Lo que no tiene nombre* (That which has no name, 2013), concerning the life and suicide in New York at the age of twenty-eight of her son Daniel, a visual artist.

RICHARD GWYN is a Welsh writer and translator, author of four collections of poetry, four novels and the memoirs *The Vagabond's Breakfast* (a Wales Book of the Year in 2012) and *Ambassador of Nowhere: A Latin American Pilgrimage* (2024), an account of his travels in search of material for *The Other Tiger: Recent Poetry from Latin America* (2016). His most recent translation is *Invisible Dog: Selected Poems of Fabio Morábito* (2024).

RIFAT ABBAS is a leading contemporary voice in Saraiki literature, with a career spanning over 40 years. A retired assistant professor, he has published poetry collections and novels which have been translated into Urdu, and has received the National Award from the Pakistan Academy of Letters numerous times. His latest book, *Muskhriyaan da Mela* ('Festival of Clowns'), will be published this year by Aks Publications.

RYAN GREENE writes and translates in Phoenix, Arizona, the city where he grew up. His most recent translations include *[INCOGNITA FLORA CUSCATLANICA]* (La Impresora, 2025) with Elena Salamanca, *Transit* (Eulalia Books, 2024) with Claudina Domingo, *[gamerover]* (Deep Vellum, 2025) with Giancarlo Huapaya, and *El ADN del canto* ('The Song's DNA', Spiral Editions, 2024) with Yaxkin Melchy.

SAMPURNA CHATTARJI's translations include Sukumar Ray's poetry and prose, *Wordygurdyboom!* (Puffin Classics, 2008), and Joy Goswami's prose poems After *Death Comes Water* (Harper Perennial, 2021). Her work as an editor includes *Future Library* (Red Hen Press, 2022), an anthology of contemporary Indian writing, released in the US. The most recent of her eleven poetry titles is *Unmappable Moves* (Poetrywala, 2023).

SANWAL GURMANI is a young emerging poet from Layyah, Pakistan, whose kafis revive the Sufi tradition with fresh lyrical energy. His work carries echoes of mystic longing, earthy wisdom, and a profound love for the Beloved, as seen in his debut book *Sadhana* ('Practice', Dastak Publications). He is currently working on his next collection, *Loonak de Phul*.

SARA ELKAMEL holds an MA in arts journalism from Columbia University and an MFA in poetry from New York University. A Pushcart Prize winner, she is the author of the poetry chapbook *Field of No Justice* (African Poetry Book Fund & Akashic Books, 2021). Her translations include Mona Kareem's chapbook, *I Will Not Fold These Maps* (Poetry Translation Centre, 2023) and Dalia Taha's *Enter World* (Graywolf Press, 2026).

STEPHEN CAPUS studied Russian at Birmingham University and The School of Slavonic and East European Studies, London University. His translations have appeared in *The Penguin Book of Russian Poetry* (Penguin, 2015) and *Centres of Cataclysm* (Bloodaxe, 2016). He has published the pamphlet *24 Hours* (Rack Press, 2020) and a selection of translations of Anna Akhmatova (Shearsman, 2025).

STEPHEN WALSH is a writer with a day-job at Christ's Hospital, Horsham, where he has worked for many years. He is the author of two travelogues for Viking Penguin, the 'warm, unusual and highly original' *Heartache Spoken Here* and the 'delightful, insightful and humorous' *Faithful Departures*. His poetry collections include *An Electorate of Turkeys* and the forthcoming *High Ball to the Wee Man*.

SUBHRO BANDOPADHYAY (1978, Calcutta, West Bengal, India) received the Indian national award for young writers (Sahitya Akademi Yuva Puraskar) in 2013 for his poetry collection *Boudho lekhomala o onyanyo shraman*. He has published four poetry collections in Spain, the latest being *Presente bajo la luz agrietada* (RIL, 2025). He teaches Spanish at Instituto Cervantes, New Delhi.

TAUQIR REZA is a multi-lingual Panjabi and Urdu poet and translator, originally from Dhunn, Chakwal, based in France. A first-generation expatriate, his work—published in the Panjabi and Urdu collections *Chann di Mitti* ('Moon Dust') and *Motiey ke Nabeena Phool* ('Jasmine's Blind Flowers')—confronts the distortions and contradictions of contemporary life. Currently, he creates book cover artwork for Modern Pakistani Literature.

YAN LI (poet and artist) was born in Beijing in 1954. He started writing poetry in 1973 and painting in 1979. He was a member of the art group Star Painting Club, and literary group Today, in Beijing in 1979, and coordinated a solo exhibition of pioneering art in China in 1984. In 1987, he founded the poetry journal *First Line New York*, where he continues to serve as editor-in-chief. He is the president of the Overseas Chinese Writers' Association.

ZSUZSA BENEY (1930–2006) trained at medical school and worked as a physician her entire life until her retirement at the age of 70. She received a PhD in literary studies in 1993, and taught poetry at several universities. In addition to nine volumes of poetry and several novels, Beney was also a highly regarded literary historian. She was the recipient of many distinguished prizes, including the Attila József Prize in 1990.

ZSUZSA RAKOVSZKY (1950–) has been translated into English by George Szirtes ('New Life', London, Oxford University Press, 1994), and her best-selling novel *Shadow of the Snake* has been translated into German, Italian, Bulgarian and Dutch. She has been awarded many prizes, including the Attila József Prize in 1988 and the Libri Literature prize in 2016. In 2009, she was made a member of the Széchenyi Academy of Literature and Arts.